Writing the Subject

American University Studies

Series XXIV
American Literature

Vol. 54

PETER LANG
New York • Washington, D.C./Baltimore • San Francisco
Bern • Frankfurt am Main • Berlin • Vienna • Paris

Gunilla Theander Kester

Writing the Subject

Bildung and
the African American Text

PETER LANG
New York • Washington, D.C./Baltimore • San Francisco
Bern • Frankfurt am Main • Berlin • Vienna • Paris

Library of Congress Cataloging-in-Publication Data

Kester, Gunilla Theander.
Writing the subject: Bildung and the African American text /
by Gunilla Theander Kester.
p. cm. — (American university studies. Series XXIV,
American literature; vol. 54)
Includes bibliographical references.
1. American fiction—Afro-American authors—History and criticism.
2. American fiction—20th century—History and criticism. 3. Postmodern
(literature)—United States. 4. Afro-Americans in literature. 5. Subjectivity in
literature. 6. Race in literature. 7. Bildungsroman. I. Title. II. Series.
PS374.N4K47   813'.5409896073—dc20   93-37319
ISBN 0-8204-2332-7 (hardcover)
ISBN 0-8204-3727-1 (paperback)
ISSN 0895-0512

Die Deutsche Bibliothek-CIP-Einheitsaufnahme

Kester, Gunilla Theander:
Writing the subject: Bildung and the African American text / by Gunilla Theander
Kester. –New York; Washington, D.C./Baltimore; Bern; Frankfurt am Main;
Berlin; Vienna; Paris: Lang.
(American university studies. Series 24, American literature; vol. 54)
ISBN 0-8204-2332-7 (hardcover)
ISBN 0-8204-3727-1 (paperback)
NE: American university studies / 24

Author photo by Jamasb Sokansanj.
Painting on the front cover by Posoon Sung.

The paper in this book meets the guidelines for permanence and durability
of the Committee on Production Guidelines for Book Longevity
of the Council of Library Resources.

Printed in the United States of America.

For Daniel, Anya, and Shiri.

ACKNOWLEDGMENTS

I want to thank my advisor, Professor J. Lee Greene, for adding depth and humor to the process of cultural understanding and for his careful and patient guidance of this project in its early stages. I would like to express my gratitude to Professor Lilian R. Furst for her encouragement. I also wish to thank Professor Eugene Falk and Professor S. K. Heninger, Jr. who opened the door to theory.

I am grateful to my editor, Heidi Burns, who calmly and competently dealt with my "Swenglish."

I also want to thank my friends who, knowingly or not, have contributed to this book in various ways: Eva Lyckegård, Maria Nyström Reuterswärd, Märit Thurborg Gaimster, Deborah Clarke, Mojdeh Karamooz, Steve Slobodski, Emmett F. Steward, Susan Kornberg, Chris Schreiner, Amy Elias, Marilyn Elkins, Andrea Kwasny, and especially Posoon Sung who made the cover for this book.

Finally, a special thank you to my parents, Sten and Siv Theander, who taught me to ask questions, and to Paul and Susanne Kester who showed me the meaning of tolerance. And, most of all, I want to thank Daniel, Anya, and Shiri Kester who mysteriously and gracefully share their lives with mine.

CONTENTS

INTRODUCTION

"it is not weakness,
— it is the contradiction of
double aims." (Du Bois 215)

The African American Narrative of *Bildung*

"What did *I* do to be so blue?" (14). At the end of the Prologue in
Ralph Ellison's *Invisible Man* (1952) the narrator offers this paraphrase of
a line from Louis Armstrong's version of the famous song lyric "Black and
Blue," but he omits the word black from the original line. Thus, with one
masterly stroke he illustrates the common erasure of the black signifier in
white Western discourse and recreates the need for a resisting black text.
Paradoxically, in suppressing one half of the description "black and blue,"
invisible man also seems to capture the very notion and reality of blackness
since, usually, such descriptions only need to be nominated when their
marginalized positions identify an un-named center. In the world of
invisible man, however, blackness is central and requires no further
identification. The invisible subject centralizes a blackness which, in turn,
indicates a different other: the white world from an African American
perspective. Alluding to a dialogic relationship—black AND blue—
invisible man also confronts a doubleness which plays a major role in
African American culture. This doubleness is one of the most distinct and
striking features of African American literature which often tends to trope
on the African American literary tradition and signify on the European
American one. Mingling memories and traditions from both cultural
spheres, African American literature can be viewed as "bilingual." It
speaks two languages. It talks a double talk. So far, much criticism on the
African American maturation novels has focused on the European
American influence and on the persistent similarities between the European
and the African American traditions. This study breaks new ground by
pointing to the profound differences between the European and the African
American views of the maturing subject and the process of *Bildung*, and by

initiating the formulation of the distinctly African American features of the genre.

The making of the dual African American identity occurs as a frequent theme in African American literature. William Edward Burghardt Du Bois formulated one of the earliest and most cogent expressions of the African American subject's double identity in *The Souls of Black Folk* (1903). The passage is well-known, yet deserves a full quotation.

> After the Egyptian and Indian, the Greek and Roman, the Teuton and Mongolian, the Negro is a sort of seventh son, born with a veil, and gifted with second-sight in this American world,—a world which yields him no true self-consciousness, but only lets him see himself through the revelation of the other world. It is a peculiar sensation, this double-consciousness, this sense of always looking at one's self through the eyes of others, of measuring one's soul by the tape of a world that looks on in amused contempt and pity. One ever feels his twoness,—an American, a Negro; two souls, two thoughts, two unreconciled strivings; two warring ideals in one dark body, whose dogged strength alone keeps it from being torn asunder.
>
> The history of the American Negro is the history of this strife,—this longing to attain self-conscious manhood, to merge his double self into a better and truer self. In this merging he wishes neither of the older selves to be lost. (214-215)

Du Bois describes a longing to merge the two halves of the African American subject and yet to retain the older selves. This study sheds light on this complex desire to overcome the pain of division but, at the same time, to keep the reasons for that pain clearly in focus. The African American double subject draws attention to the limits between cultures and highlights the division between textuality and history. Historically, the African American identity is double, forged out of the enforced and violent confrontation between two cultural spheres, the African and the European. It is an identity written in blood. In *The Autobiography of an Ex-Coloured Man* (1912) James Weldon Johnson's protagonist illuminates the consequences of that history and the internalization of its power structure when he describes the day he first understood that he was an African American.

> From that time I looked out through other eyes, my thoughts were coloured, my words dictated, my actions limited by one dominating, all-pervading idea which constantly increased in force and weight until I finally realized in it a great, tangible fact.
>
> And this is the dwarfing, warping, distorting influence which operates upon each and every coloured man in the United States. He is forced to take his outlook on all things, not from the view-point of a citizen, or a man, or even a human being, but from the view-point of a *coloured* man . . . . This gives to every coloured man, in proportion to his intellectuality, a sort of dual personality . . . (403)

But the African American subject is also an exploration of textual possibilities and the limits between text and world. In modern African American literature the concern with double identity and the constant struggle against adopting a surrounding culture's negative views of blackness often takes the shape of a discourse of clothing. Toni Morrison's *The Bluest Eye* (1970) remains the most wrenching account of the processes of internalizing self-deprecatory views which she describes as a cloaking of the self. The narrator thinks that the Breedloves are ugly because they believe that they are ugly.

> You looked at them and wondered why they were so ugly; you looked closely and could not find the source. Then you realized that it came from conviction, their conviction. It was as though some mysterious all-knowing master had given each one a cloak of ugliness to wear, and they had each accepted it without question. The master had said, "You are ugly people." They had looked about themselves and saw nothing to contradict the statement; saw, in fact, support for it leaning at them from every billboard, every movie, every glance. "Yes," they had said. "You are right." And

they took the ugliness in their hand, threw it as a mantle over them, and
went about the world with it. (34)

The image of doubleness as a sort of clothing reappears when Pecola
wears it as a "shroud" (35) and the community shapes its response to her
behind a "veil." With a possible allusion to the famous passage from Du
Bois, the narrator describes the indifference of her community as a hiding
behind veils: "we listened for the one who would say, 'Poor little girl,' or,
'Poor baby,' but there was only head-wagging where those words should
have been. We looked for eyes creased with concern, but saw only veils"
(148). Symbolically, these veils mark a division within which could hide a
different, possibly a more compassionate, response for Pecola's fate. But
regardless of the interpretation, the veils inscribe a doubleness. In *Give
Birth to Brightness* (1972), Sherley Anne Williams explores the similarly
double position of the hero in Neo-Black literature.

It is, of course, an exaggeration to say that the Black villain in the white
community is the hero of the Black community. Rather, it is more accurate
to say that a hero in the eyes of Black people is more likely to be a
law breaker than a law-maker. Beyond the simple fact that it is only
recently that even a small number of Black people have been in a position to
affect and effect rules which touch the lives of Blacks, is the deeper, more
significant fact that laws have been used more as instruments for the
oppression of Black people than as means to serve or protect them. And,
where the judicial system has been lax in controlling Blacks, social customs
have taken up the slack. Thus, obtaining the dominant society's approval
for public or private actions has not been, for Blacks, to obey the laws and
be considered a respectable, law-abiding man, but to obey the laws and be
praised as a good nigger. It is thus almost axiomatic that good niggers
cannot be heroes, for heroes affirm through their actions not only the values
of their culture but also their personal worth in their own eyes. The Black
man, in being one, must always fail in the other. American history provides
glaring instances in which Blacks have sought a white-defined heroism only
to find that they have negated their own humanity. (213)

In being one, the black hero must fail in the other. Showing how the African American subject is judged from two cultural perspectives at the same time, Williams renders a most succinct description of the African American subject's double position. Morrison and Williams describe a doubleness which is neither within nor without, and they show how the African American expressions of doubleness permeate all aspects of the African American subject.

The theme of masking is one common expression of this doubleness in African American literature and folk culture. But in my view the double nature of African American literature goes beyond thematic concerns. Structurally, the double identity is often reflected in the dual subject who is both teller of the story and its protagonist. The first person narrators in the slave narratives as well as the self-producing narrating subjects in many modern African American novels exemplify the structural doubleness of African American literature and require a double analysis of both *fabula* and *sjuzet*, both discourse and story. This doubleness may not seem to differ in any important way from that of all first person narratives, but the immersion of doubleness on all levels of African American culture raises its connotative power into a category of its own. Most significantly, the doubleness of the African American subject provokes persistent questions about the relationship between subjectivity and language. This relationship widens the analysis from one designed to deal primarily with the formal coding of the texts to one designed to incorporate the social, historical "coding" of the subjects as well. It shows that the doubleness is neither "within" nor "without," but highlights and transcends such limits. A main focus is given to the limit between art and world, between textuality and history. Since both world and history can only be known through text, the aim is to push world and history to the limits of text and possibly beyond. This way the African American narrative of *Bildung* attempts to create a space for the subject of history in the world thus to enable and empower the African American double subject in the world and in history.

The African American narrative of *Bildung*, like the slave narrative and the classical *Bildungsroman*, describes the relationship between an individual and his or her world. As Du Bois and Johnson so cogently state, in the African American narrative of *Bildung* this relationship is double. In his *Narrative of the Life of Frederick Douglass, an American Slave. Written by Himself* (1845), Douglass identifies one major reason for the doubleness of the African American subject. Finding it impossible to separate his individual fate from the fate of all of his people, Douglass vacillates between writing a personal history and a representational history. As much as he tries to shape his life on his own, at times mocking the folk tradition, he returns in the *Narrative of the Life* to his folk at all major moments of change. This need to present and to represent a double subject, to write both one's personal and representational identity, permeates the African American literary tradition from the earliest slave narratives to recent publications by African American authors. To write the double African American subject is necessary. The urge crystallizes against the historical background of the time of enslavement of black people in America, a time during which white laws forbade anyone to teach slaves to read and write. Exclusion from the written word, and thus also from all historical records, was a major part of the intricate power structure that white people constructed in order effectively to exploit black people and to ensure the continuance of an extremely profitable system for whites. Therefore, the struggle for literacy and the production of a written—both personal and representational—history have always been a part of the rich texture of African American culture, and it has always been a revolutionary, political act.

This continuing struggle for the right to define one's own subjectivity, the identity of the race, and the world from a black perspective has created within the African American literary tradition an unprecedented awareness of the power of textuality in shaping identities. The knowledge that an unwritten reality is in a sense invisible, transparent, and easily overlooked runs deep in the African American cultural memory, and it has informed the desire to produce the novels which I will discuss. Ralph Ellison's *Invisible Man*, Toni Morrison's *The Bluest Eye*, Gayl Jones' *Eva's Man* (1976), Charles Johnson's *Oxherding Tale* (1982), and Sherley Anne Williams' *Dessa Rose* (1986) are all fictitious first person narratives which, in various ways, recount the process of growing up black and male or black and female in America. These novels may all include autobiographical elements, but they cannot be classified as autobiography. Rather, since all these novels are stories about maturation and coming-of-age, they must be viewed as *Bildungsromane*.

The German term *Bildungsroman*, however, comes with a historical baggage of associations to positivism, white male superiority, and a sense of the self as a unified entity. This baggage often conflicts with the African American tradition. Wilhelm Dilthey's famous definition of the *Bildungsroman* demonstrates how anathema and inappropriate the term is in relation to African American ways of writing the subject. He defines the classical *Bildungsroman* as a novel in which a "regulated development within the life of the individual is observed, each of its stages has its own intrinsic value and is at the same time the basis for a higher stage. The dissonances and conflicts of life appear as the necessary growth points through which the individual must pass on his way to maturity and harmony."[1] Similarly, Eric Blackall calls Johann Wolfgang von Goethe's *Wilhelm Meister*, the prototypical hero of the classical *Bildungsroman*, "a seeker for some whole, some community outside himself in which his individual existence will be meaningful and productive."[2] In her article on the novel of formation as genre, Marianne Hirsch compares the *Bildungsroman* to the picaresque novel and the confessional novel, concluding that "In contrast to both these related forms, the novel of formation is founded on the belief in progress and the coherence of selfhood."[3] In his famous study on the development of the *Bildungsroman*, Michael Beddow argues that "what is happening in the text is guided by the maxims of the Society of the Tower. Viewed from the perspective offered by those maxims, Wilhelm's superficially wayward and inconsequential history of errors and perplexities figures as the inevitably complex and apparently untidy process of clarification and expression of the immanent form of his unique personality, and of the concrete possibilities of bringing that personality into fruitful engagement with the outer world available to him."[4] Clearly, the classical *Bildungsroman* strives to inscribe a view of the subject as a unified and singular identity. It proposes the growth of a subject from one fixed state of mind to another: immaturity and maturity. It also implies a sense of progression. These associations began to accumulate with Wieland and Goethe and have grown heavier since. They clearly clash with the African American agenda, experience, and ideology, and they indicate that the African American narrative of *Bildung* is a different genre that must be separated from the European one.

In an attempt, therefore, to separate the traveler and the luggage, I prefer to call these novels African American "narratives of *Bildung*." I choose to retain the German word *Bildung* because there is not a precise English translation for it. English uses several different labels in an attempt to capture the many aspects of the German expression. For instance, when one focuses on the psychological aspects of a novel of this type, one speaks of the maturation, the rite of spring, or the coming-of-age novel; when one is more interested in social aspects of the narrative, one uses phrases such as the novel of education, the apprenticeship novel, or the cultivation novel. The fact is that all of these descriptive labels and qualities in their English forms inhere in the German term *Bildung*, for *Bildung* embodies a double process of inner developing and outer enveloping, what the Germans call *Anbildung* and *Ausbildung*. On the one hand, the word *Bildung* describes how the strengths and talents of the individual emerge, a development of the individual; on the other hand, *Bildung* also describes how the individual's society uses well the individual's manifest strengths and talents, a social "enveloping" of the individual. The maturation processes discussed in the following pages clearly depict societies which ignore their responsibilities of "enveloping" and the subjects' desperate attempts to "develop" in spite of racial and gendered oppression.

The novels I discuss in this study also can be classified more narrowly as "modern narratives of *Bildung*," since they, in the words of Robert Stepto, "revoice their antecedent narratives" (96). For the purposes in this study, the "antecedent narratives" include both European and African American predecessors. The modern African American narratives of *Bildung* are heirs to and trope on the great slave narrative tradition, and they also revoice or signify on the European American tradition of

Bildung. But this equation between texts and literary generations never adds up. There is too much slippage, spillage, splitting, and excess. Each text remains as independent and as dependent as the other. These differences and similarities belong to history and to structure, and it is quite possible that this system is arbitrary.

Because they partake in a specifically American suspicion against organized society, these novels also, in a general sense, can be seen as "American narratives of *Bildung*." The most striking difference between the European and the American narratives of *Bildung* lies in the portrayal of society, which is often radically different in the American maturation stories. In Goethe's *Wilhelm Meisters Lehrjahre* or, in English, *Wilhelm Meister's Years of Apprenticeship* (1795-96; 1829 final version) and most other European *Bildungsromane* society is usually depicted as a benevolent force which envelopes the worthy individual with care. In contrast, both African American and European American literature often represents society negatively. In European American narratives of *Bildung* such as *Huckleberry Finn*, *Moby-Dick*, *The Sound and the Fury*, *A Farewell to Arms*, *The Catcher in the Rye*, *In Country*, and *Housekeeping*, to mention a few, the authors often portray American society as arbitrary, anti-individual, unjust, and cruel. In African American narratives of *Bildung* such as *The Autobiography of an Ex-Coloured Man*, *Their Eyes Were Watching God*, *Black Boy*, *Native Son*, *Go Tell It On the Mountain*, *The Color Purple*, the forces of society are usually projected as less arbitrary, but equally, if not more, cruel and unjust.

In a general sense, the novels in this study are modern and American, but they must first and foremost be classified as African American narratives of *Bildung*. Each novel is uniquely shaped, but they share a historical and a literary doubleness as well as a sense of the subject as a divided phenomenon. This doubleness of the African American narrative of *Bildung* must be distinguished from the dialectic element within the German *Bildungsroman*. The duality within that genre has been variously described at different times. Goethe's contemporaries reacted against the artificiality of the form combined with what seemed to them the most natural of all processes, that of growing up. The Romantics, on the other hand, cheered the ideal of the development of the whole human soul in all its interesting variations, but they dreaded the ending of the process which almost always contained marriage and a return to a quite narrow bourgeois existence.[5] In discussing the German *Bildungsroman* from Wieland to Hesse, Swales sees the generic tension as a reflection of the interest in history in the *Humanitätsideal* of late eighteenth-century Germany. He argues that "It is indeed at the intersection of story (history) and mind (idea) that the Bildungsroman will generate its characteristic import, one which evolves out of an artistically controlled, and frequently unresolved, tension" (17). Patricia Alden on the other hand discusses the dialectic within the genre by emphasizing the double bind noticeable in nineteenth- and twentieth-century British versions of the narrative of *Bildung* in such texts as *Born in Exile*, *Jude the Obscure*, *Clayhanger*, *Sons and Lovers*, and *The Rainbow*. She argues that "These are significant reworkings of the Bildungsroman which had projected the harmonious integration of the individual into a social and material culture supportive of his development. Instead these writers find only the possibility of self-betrayal which leads to disintegration of self, an overwhelming sense of the powerlessness of the individual to effect his development, and a complete rupture between self and society" (4). In *The Way of the World*, Franco Moretti also emphasizes the sense of duality in the classical *Bildungsroman* as he identifies the inherent contradiction between the two opposing ideals in the classical *Bildungsroman*, youth and maturity, as well as "the conflict between the ideal of *self-determination* and the equally imperious demands of *socialization*" (15). Yet, the classical genre strives to resolve the contradiction between world and self; in a Kantian fashion, the imagination of the mature subject can overcome the restrictions of the world and thus obtain a sense of harmony. Compromise, Franco Moretti argues, is "the novel's most celebrated theme" (9). The dissolution of contradiction at the end of the classical genre stands in stark contrast to the African American narrative of *Bildung* in which the maturing subject learns to recognize his or her double identity and to realize that, in a sense, a divided subject has no identity. Such a double subject cannot, like the classical protagonist, be both origin and *telos* of the story and of the world it describes.[6]

The African American double subject and his or her world do not fuse together in a harmonious whole at the end of the novels.   Rather, the African American narrative of *Bildung* often questions the whole notion of closure.   It tends to confront textuality with worldliness in a way that forces the reader to leap from the literary realm to the dimension of the real.   The 1993 Nobel Laureate for Literature Toni Morrison has commented on the "quality of hunger and disturbance [in the spiritual and in jazz] that never ends . . . Jazz always keeps you on the edge. There is no final chord. . . . a long chord, but no final chord."[7] Nellie McKay remarks that "Emotional closure, she [Morrison] thinks, is not compatible with the black artistic sensibility" (1).   The African American narrative of *Bildung* shifts the focus away from a teleological thrust which separates art from life in the classical European and European American tradition to an engaged response which fuses art and life.   This new focus indicates an attempt to negotiate a contact between literature and reality, art and history.   This desire to write a non-Aristotelian text with endings which both invite and demand changes in the historical process has a profound impact on all aspects of the African American doubleness.   The focus on the limits between textuality and history creates a recognition of the difference between written and lived experience and adds a sense of distance between what was read and what can be done.   It provokes a sense of agency, then, based on the "doubling" of the text in the dimension of the real.   The writing of the subject is in this sense a utopian project; a wish, a dream, a code, a structure, and a tool for the future.   The writing of the subject is a process of erasing what is being written to free a possible agency outside of the text.

Language and the Subject

African American literature creatively expresses the consequences of the enforced dislocation and the continued search for a sense of self in the diaspora.   It was my wish to trace and describe the African American system of writing the subject as it was exemplified in five contemporary

African American novels. I wanted to recognize the unique features of the African American subject which—forged from a singularly brutal history—sharply distinguished it from white Western ways of presenting selfhood. But I soon realized the relevance of these features to the recent aggressive debate about subjectivity in contemporary philosophy and theory. My aim for studying the African American subject then became twofold. On the one hand I tried to understand the differences between African American and European systems of writing the subject. On the other hand, I tried to resist the temptation to essentialize the topic. It is my belief that a proper understanding of the African American subject can contribute to and enlighten the discussion about the poststructuralist and the postmodernist subject; it is my hope that, in some ways, poststructuralism and postmodernism can shed light on the African American subject.

Poststructuralists and postmodernists have battered the old notion of the unified subject, the individual identity, on all fronts, relating subject formation to semiotics. Structuralist and poststructuralist investigations into the nature of text effectively deny the possibility of agency in the subject as well as its old position as both origin and *telos* of meaning. *"There is nothing outside of the text [there is no outside-text; il n'y a de hors-texte]"* (1976: 158). Jacques Derrida's famous formulation places the context of meaning inside a system neither an author nor an interpreter can control or dominate. Within this system, referents such as world and the subject, reality and individuality, history and fiction, become irrelevant because the focus is no longer to "double" the text at hand, but to open its "signifying structure." Even though a text may seem to rely on reality as a model, this approach demonstrates its adherence to a system of signifying which is part of increasingly larger textual contexts. Rather than expecting the text to double reality, "reality" seems to copy the textual system of signifying. In *Language and Materialism: Developments in Semiology and the Theory of the Subject* Rosalind Coward and John Ellis argue that "all social practices can be understood as meanings, as signification and as circuits of exchange between subjects, and therefore can lean on linguistics as a model for the elaboration of their systematic reality."

Because all the practices that make up a social totality take place in language, it becomes possible to consider language as the place in which the social individual is constructed. In other words, man can be seen *as language*, as the intersection of the social, historical and individual. It is for this reason that work on language has created consideration of man as 'subject', [sic] that is, the individual in sociality as a language-using, social and historical entity. (1)

This possibility that reality will copy or double the text is a strong component in the African American narrative of *Bildung*. It tries to expose the limits between text and reality to facilitate the leap from literature to history. The aim of this process of doubling is revolutionary.

The writing of the subject is a compositional process which arranges textual hierarchies in ways which no individual can control; readings of that subject can, however, throw light on the patterns of domination it reveals. The structures of race and gender and the social consequences of slavery are encoded in the writing of the African American subject and make its features distinct. The unique traits of African American literature is further increased through a theory which is based on the African American vehicles of the vernacular—the myths, the folklore, and the stories from Africa and America, the blues and the spirituals. Houston Baker explains how "the relentless tendency" of theory is "to go beyond the tangible in search of a metalevel of explanation," and how the history of African Americans has produced a specific double theoretical outlook.

Africans uprooted from ancestral soil, stripped of material culture, and victimized by brutal contact with various European nations were compelled not only to maintain their cultural heritage at a *meta* (as opposed to a material) level, but also to apprehend the operative metaphysics of various alien cultures. ("There is No More" 135)

The African American production of theory, as it is expressed in these African American narratives of *Bildung*, often rearranges relationships between theoretical categories as they have been described in European and

European American theory. These differences do not necessarily render the categories invalid, but it cautions the reader not to link the different poststructuralist texts too quickly.

The highly self-conscious exploration into the notion of subjectivity as a double discourse can be found not only within African American culture, but also in postmodernist theory and practice. Postmodernism? There are today many descriptions of the postmodernist épistémé; still, ontologically and epistemologically there is little agreement about what postmodernism really is or what to think of it. Is it a literary period or a type of literature? Is it a development of modernism or a reaction against it? Is it a cultural paradigm or a social and political reality? Is it bad or good, frightening or inspiring? The critical community disagrees. Yet, for all the differing opinions, both conservative and radical critics of postmodernism focus on the status of the subject, the-once-upon-a-time coherent Cartesian *cogito*, the centered bourgeois ego. For example, Gerald Graff argues that postmodernism is characterized by "a dissolution of ego boundaries" (57); Daniel Bell that "the various kinds of postmodernism . . . are simply the decomposition of the self in an effort to erase the individual ego" (29). While Ihab Hassan maintains that "the Self . . . is really an empty 'place' where many selves come to mingle and depart" (1977: 845), Hans Bertens thinks that the "postmodern self is no longer a coherent entity that has the power to impose (admittedly subjective) order upon its environment" (47). Likewise, Fredric Jameson posits that "the old individual or individualist subject is 'dead'" (Kaplan 17), while George Yúdice maintains that the postmodernist "revolution" entails "an unceasing dissolution of the (Western) subject" (218).

The urgency of the conflict between political engagement and the decentering of the subject has been most strongly felt in discourses of oppressed minorities and decolonialized people as well as in feminist theory and praxis. In her recent study on feminism and postmodernism, Patricia Waugh explains how "Postmodernism expresses nostalgia for but loss of belief in the concept of the human subject as an agent effectively intervening in history, through its fragmentation of discourses, language games, and decentering of subjectivity. Feminism seeks a subjective identity, a sense of effective agency and history for women which has hitherto been denied them by the dominant culture" (9). In *Engendering the Subject*, Sally Robinson solves this conflict by splitting the female subject into "Woman" versus "women." She argues that "the differences between Woman and women get at the heart of the contradictions that feminist theory is grappling with at the present moment: the general and systematic versus the specific and local; the negativity of critique versus the positivity of transformative politics; unified identity versus situational identities; the sexual difference versus multiplicitous gender differences" (9). Robinson's strategy keenly identifies an ideological and practical dilemma in the discourses of the oppressed and presents a possible route beyond it through learning new ways of writing and reading the subject. Although I have resisted adopting a description of the subject as dichotomy, the vacillation between the local and the systematic is certainly present in the following pages.

In *Decolonizing the Mind* Ngugi Wa Thiong'o writes about how language shapes images of ourselves and the world and how "our capacity to confront the world creatively is dependent on how those images correspond or not to that reality, how they distort or clarify the reality of our struggles. . . . Language is mediating in my very being"(15). From this standpoint, the erasure of the (Western) subject must appear premature at best, but maybe also premeditated. An early closure of this debate could be a way to silence different views about history, power, and self representation, so as to slow change and strengthen status quo. Abdul R. JanMohamed argues that the "most crucial aspect of resisting the hegemony consists in struggling against its attempt to form one's subjectivity, for it is through the construction of the minority subject that the dominant culture can elicit the individual's own help in his/her oppression. One of the most powerful weapons in the hands of the oppressor is the mind of the oppressed; without control of the latter's mind the dominant culture can enforce compliance only through the constant use of brute force" (104). This context clarifies the progressive note of the resistance to the dissolution of the subject in minority discourse. While most European American postmodernist critics either lament or celebrate the death of the subject, African American authors explore a different kind of subjectivity which is contingent, collective, and historical.[8] Seeking its unique position, this subject is part lack, part desire. It relates to what is lost, the absent African home continent, and to what still seems unavailable to many African Americans, a home on the American continent. In contrast to the European American subject, the African American subject engages in a dialogue between reference and reflexivity. It opens a new space for exploring the issue of history, of a shared experience of exploitation, and its relationship to the literary testimonies of that history.

The double allegiance to fact and fiction is one important feature of the doubleness in the African American narrative of *Bildung*. In a similar way, the modern African American narratives of *Bildung* talk a complex double talk with their literary antecedents. The European corpuscular-kinetic subject was grounded in individualism and universalism. Built on violence and exclusion, it has made many people blind to otherness. Now, it faces challenges on several fronts. In various cultural contexts, a different and contingent picture of the subject is emerging. Its features may still seem vague and difficult to interpret, especially for those of us who are steeped in a European and a European American tradition, but its characteristics also become more distinct when seen against the backdrop of the European American tradition. Therefore, this study begins with two comparative chapters. Chapter one focuses on the much debated relationship between *Notes from Underground* and *Invisible Man*. Many critics have noticed the formal similarities of the two novels, but I concentrate on the striking differences between the two subjects which may also capture a difference between modernist and postmodernist views of subjectivity. Chapter two illuminates the double heritage of the African American narrative of *Bildung*, a direct heritage from the slave narratives and an indirect one from the classical *Bildungsroman*. This chapter compares *Invisible Man* to Frederick Douglass' *Narrative of the Life* and to Johann Wolfgang von Goethe's *Wilhelm Meister*. In *The Signifying Monkey* (1989) Henry Louis Gates makes a distinction between "signifying" as he used the term in *Figures in Black* (1987) and "Signifyin(g)" as the concept derives from African and African American vernacular culture. This chapter illustrates Gates' distinction in that it shows how *Invisible Man* tropes, or Signifies, on the African American slave narrative while it reverses or signifies on the German classical *Bildungsroman*. The traits that most separate the modern African American narratives of *Bildung* from the classical, German *Bildungsroman* often are part of the inheritance from the slave narrative tradition. Typically, the classical *Bildungsroman* is a chronological, linear, third person narrative, which also is white, male, Western, and with a distinct positivistic bias. In contrast, the African American narrative of *Bildung* is told in first person, contains a disruption in the chronology of events, and it is told by African American men, women, and children whose views of subjectivity prompts them to replace the notion of individuality with a collective, "trans-individual subject" (the phrase is Lucien Goldmann's).

Chapter three explores the endeavors of two female African American subjects who invent a double textual code in which to express themselves. Toni Morrison's *The Bluest Eye* and Gayl Jones' *Eva's Man* share three noticeable features: a desolate and destructive tale of a sexually violated girl, an intricate language and structure, and a concern with the boundary between the eye of the subject and the gaze of the other, both connected to the mute, silenced female subject. *Eva's Man* and *The Bluest Eye* contrast male power and desire to female suppression of both impulses, and they illustrate the actual terror behind the postmodernist subject position. In discussing postmodernist processes of subject formation John Johnston proposes that

> the postmodern subject passes through two related forms of subjection: one consists in a form of individuation shaped by the demands of power, the other in a fixing of each individual with a known, stable identity, well determined once and for all, through a channeling of desire. In response to these two forms of subjection, postmodern subjectivity—since there is no self-identical "postmodern subject" per se—presents itself as the right to difference, to variation, and to metamorphosis. (71)

Johnston's definition of the postmodernist subjectivity illustrates how deeply ingrained the tendency to see the subject as an agent remains even in postmodernist and poststructuralist thinking. In contrast, the passivity, victimization, and lacking female resistant text in Jones' and Morrison's novels clearly show the horror of "the dissolution of self". The only way to explore a constructive narrative of *Bildung* in these two novels is through the countering force of text. Eva creates a diegetic cure in *Eva's Man*. Pecola does not tell her own story, but she, too, becomes a kind of narrating subject when, near the end of the novel, she creates dialogues in her mind. Both of them participate in the process of structuring the female African American subject. They discover ways of splitting their experiences into a metaphorical and a metonymical code. Through uses of metonymy, they contrast the male-dominated world that victimizes them to a different world in which they can begin to formulate their female subjectivity, which they produce metaphorically. Through a double textual code, they produce a space for difference and a possibility of change.

If, however, the African American narrating subjects measure their sense of identity against the structures of race and gender, they also tend to balance their sense of freedom with the material world around them. Chapter four highlights two novels about the transition from slavery to freedom—Charles Johnson's *Oxherding Tale* and Sherley Anne Williams' *Dessa Rose*. Both of these novels present a double pursuit of freedom. On the one hand, both narrating subjects are seeking material freedom from an economic system that exploits them as slaves. On the other hand, they need to complement the pursuit of material freedom with an exploration of the racial tropes which contribute to the stability of that system. In *Oxherding Tale* the mysterious character the Soulcatcher illustrates and transforms both symbolic and metaphoric representations of blackness. In *Dessa Rose* Rufel and Dessa quarrel about a figure they both refer to as "Mammy." The white woman's "Mammy" transcends blackness while the black woman's "Mammy" deepens the significance of blackness. In my view this scene offers a critique of both symbolic and metaphoric tropes for blackness. The lack of a referent also reverses the order between the symbolic and the semiotic: in order to pursue freedom both women need to escape a symbolic order from which they have been excluded.

The conclusion states theoretically how the subject formation in the African American narrative of *Bildung* anticipates a postmodernist reformulation of that genre. In the Introduction to *Postmodern Genres*, Marjorie Perloff writes that "It is the paradox of postmodern genre that the more radical the dissolution of traditional generic boundaries, the more important the concept of genericity becomes" (4). In view of how popular it is to apply the term *Bildungsroman* to African American narratives of *Bildung*, the conclusion to this study theorizes the major differences between the two. In contrast to the image of the subject as a fairly stable and unified self in the classical *Bildungsroman*, the African American narrative of *Bildung* projects a double subject. In order to explicate this image of the subject, I propose an analogy between the African American double subject and the semiotic sign. There is also a fundamental difference in the overall order or progression of the presentation of the subject in the two traditions. The classical *Bildungsroman* projects the subject in a specific order. First, it posits the being of the subject as something outside of the textual realm. Then it posits the author-narrator as someone who can actually see that subject in a moment of phenomenological truth. When these two steps are completed, the controlled and authoritarian process of producing a replica of that subject in text can begin. The African American narrative of *Bildung*, however, reverses the order of these steps. Invisible man, for example, begins by signifying. Claiming no other existence than as textual construct, the narrator of *Invisible Man* is in no way separated from his creation. The binary opposition between inner and outer, real and related, past and present truth, collapses. The subject and his or her world no longer master the narrative portrait; instead, the textual production of subject and world determines their existence. In this sense, all these novels illustrate Du Bois' wish to merge the double self into "a better and truer self" without losing the older selves.

NOTES

1 Quoted by Martin Swales in *The German Bildungsroman from Wieland to Hesse* (Princeton, N.J.: Princeton UP, 1978) 3.
2 *Goethe and the Novel* (Ithaca: Cornell UP, 1976) 62.
3 "The Novel of Formation as Genre: Between Great Expectations and Lost Illusions," *Genre* 12 (1979): 293-311. See p. 299.
4 *The Fiction of Humanity: Studies in the Bildungsroman from Wieland to Thomas Mann* (Cambridge: Cambridge UP, 1982) 125-126. See also Patricia Alden's *Social Mobility in the English Bildungsroman: Gissing, Hardy, Bennett, and Lawrence* (Ann Arbor: UMI Research P, 1986).
5 For an excellent historical overview, see Martin Swales' chapter "Bildungsroman as Genre."
6 In contrast to the Male-Female Double *Bildungsroman*, the African American double narrative of *Bildung* describes a split within the subject, not a split between an active, socially successful male protagonist and a passive, victimized female one. See Charlotte Goodman, "The Lost Brother, The Twin: Women Novelists and The Male-Female Double *Bildungsroman*," *Novel* 17 (1983): 28-43.
7 Quoted by Nellie Y. McKay in the Introduction to *Critical Essays on Toni Morrison* (Boston: G.K. Hall, 1988) 1.
8 Bonnie Hoover Braendlin also makes this point. Her conclusion is that "Those who mourn the demise of the *Bildungsroman* and, more generally, the 'loss' of the self in the twentieth century fail to look beyond the literary mainstream, beyond the patriarchal, white male system" (86). Quoted from *Denver Quarterly* 17. 4 (1983): 75-87.

1

The African American Double Subject:
Ralph Ellison's *Invisible Man*

"I think all good art has always been political."
(Toni Morrison, *Conversations*, 3)

"Producing, a product: a producing/product identity."
(*Anti-Oedipus*)

It is tempting to call Ralph Ellison's *Invisible Man* the most outstanding, complex, and representative African American narrative of *Bildung* of this century. The novel has often been referred to as a *Bildungsroman* since it narrates the making of an invisible man.[1] It describes the maturation process of a young black man who grows up in a race-divided society and whose search for an African American identity takes him through various schools, jobs, and political or religious institutions. This rather straightforward and chronological part of the novel is framed by a Prologue and an Epilogue which, like a talking drum or a Greek chorus, comment on the main part of the story. This textual frame prepares, underlines, and undermines the impressions formed by the tale proper and adds to its symbolic strength. The framing device also curbs the tale and calls into question whether growth and maturation are linear and chronological developments. In addition, the frame activates the paradoxical nature of all textual events as commentary on other textual events. The ever widening gyre of textuality has rendered futile the search for the beginning, middle, and end of events and problematized the status of the literary subject. This situation gets even more complex when the subject belongs to a minority culture and develops in relationship to two culturally diverse traditions. The double subject is created with the awareness that it will be judged and understood from two cultural perspectives at the same time.

The perception, production, and reception of the subject in the African American novel is rooted in its history and suggestive of a texture different from many subjects in the European and the European American traditions. At the same time, the identity of the double subject may be perceived in relief against the backdrop of Western discourse. *Invisible Man* was written in dialogue with the Western tradition. Ralph Ellison thought so and most critics who have done so-called influence studies have agreed. Ellison himself mentions that he drew on a number of white writers such as Joyce, Eliot, Hemingway, Dante, Dostoevsky, and Malraux.[2] The scope of this chapter does not permit a thorough discussion of the intertextual quality of *Invisible Man*, which has been well documented elsewhere.[3] Instead, it focuses on the differences between the dialectic subject of the classical *Bildungsroman* and the dialogic subject in the modernist European *Bildungsroman* and the double subject of the African American narrative of *Bildung*. As illusive and temporary as such distinctions tend to be, invisible man attempts to define not so much himself as the blackness that defines him. Having to face and often to respond to a series of stereotypical and racist definitions of who he is and should be from both the dominant culture and the black community, invisible man finds that blackness is and blackness "aint." Invoking the doubleness and the reversibility of the linguistic sign, invisible man shows that blackness is a culturally double construct and system of representation. Treating blackness and subjectivity in non-essentialist ways brings with it the issue of closure which trails every discourse of the sign and which has been central in the theory and praxis of African American culture. In his book *Keeping Faith* Cornel West suggests that the African American subject is not yet born, that centuries of oppression has created a namelessness and invisibility which is yet to be overcome, and that this is the progressive challenge of, what he calls, the New World African. Often shaped or even distorted by exile, exploitation, brutality, and commodification, the black Other searches for a sense of self which is not determined from without. The doubleness and reversibility of its structure is therefore often produced as difference and distance rather than as identification and sameness. In contrast, the European *Bildungsroman* outlines the subject in terms of longing for sameness and identification. The dialectic subject in the classical *Bildungsroman* strives toward an identification with the social system, and the dialogic subject in Dostoevsky's *Notes from Underground* turns away from society toward increased self-sufficiency and self-identification. Being consistently denied a reasonable sense of citizenship, the African American subject seems instead to represent its double split identity in order to produce the culturally double readings necessary for cultural survival and transformation.

The subsequent discussion highlights the differences between the dialectic, the dialogic, and the double representations of the subject and links them to the discussion on the subject in modernist and postmodernist discourse. Of course, the use of any such terms will in some ways narrow the scope of the artistic vision and provoke feelings of dissatisfaction and disagreement among readers. In part, these reactions stem from the lack of agreement on how to define modernism and postmodernism and how to perceive the relationship between the two. I use the word modern to describe all reformulations of the classical *Bildungsroman*, all texts which, in Robert Stepto's phrase, "revoice their antecedent narratives" (96). In addition, for the sake of clarity, I draw a rather sharp and, at times, unsatisfactory distinction between modernist and postmodernist subjectivity. Briefly put, I have called the underground man "modernist" because he projects and enlarges his individual uniqueness and consequently cuts himself off from the struggles of his contemporaries. Invisible man, on the other hand, creates a contingent sense of self which allows him to partake in the struggles of people everywhere. This engaged response with the world has been co-opted into the more radical factions of postmodernism, but invisible man was one of its earliest and most subtle spokespersons; he not only clarified its features but also cemented its strong connection to the minority experience. In this sense, invisible man may be more properly described as postcolonial.

Invisible man can also be seen as postmodern because he calls into question the, in the West, traditional boundaries of a novel. Teasing the reader who attempts to find a starting point from which to understand the blackness which separates his narrative of *Bildung* from the white precursors of that genre, he proclaims that the end is in the beginning. The end of what? The beginning of what? The story? The experience it describes? The history it alludes to? Invisible man's blackness provides one natural starting point; as an African American protagonist he differs from most protagonists in the tradition of the *Bildungsroman*. History provides another starting point since the deracination from Africa, the Middle Passage, and the institution of slavery must be an essential part of any African American narrative of *Bildung*. But invisible man also makes it clear that, as he puts it, he is not a freak either of nature or of history. On the one hand, a product of natural and historical circumstances, he is certainly no "freak." On the other hand, nature and history alone cannot explain his identity. A literary event, invisible man is also an exploration of the experiences and consequences of doubleness. Constructed against the backdrop of Western discourse, it takes the reader on a voyage through the history of a young man and of his people; in the process, it formulates one of the strongest narratives of the African American double and postmodernist subject.[4]

The Image of the Cave and the Double Subject

If *Invisible Man* is one of the best African American narratives of *Bildung* of this century, it also provides an unusually sensual and sophisticated rhetoric of the African American double subject which illuminates the relations between nature and history, subjectivity and textuality. Describing a dream in the Prologue section, invisible man uses symbolic language to give the reader a clue to the complexity of his vision. Smoking a joint he listens to Louis Armstrong's version of the song "Black and Blue" and begins to appreciate music not only temporally but spatially as well.[5] In order to communicate his spatial experience, invisible man describes a cave with three levels. The quotation is long, but it captures the core of the double subject and must be read in its totality.

That night I found myself hearing not only in time, but in space as well. I not only entered the music but descended, like Dante, into its depths. And *beneath the swiftness of the hot tempo there was a slower tempo and a cave and I entered it and looked around and heard an old woman singing a spiritual as full of Weltschmerz as flamenco, and beneath that lay a still lower level on which I saw a beautiful girl the color of ivory pleading in a voice like my mother's as she stood before a group of slaveowners who bid for her naked body, and below that I found a lower level and a more rapid tempo and I heard someone shout:*

"Brothers and sisters, my text this morning is the 'Blackness of Blackness'." (8-9)

High on marijuana and music invisible man descends into the cave and describes what is happening on each level. On the first level, an old woman sings a spiritual; on the second, a young woman is pleading with slaveowners; and on the third, a preacher is preaching a text he calls the "Blackness of Blackness." This tripartite image could be read as a rhetoric, a practical handbook on how to approach invisible man's formulation of the double subject. The three levels of the cave can be viewed as three different, interdependent stages all of which must be part of the African American subject. The first step corresponds to the old woman singing a spiritual full of *Weltschmerz*, an image which, even though the woman expresses it through the black vehicle of the spiritual, evokes the universal suffering of humankind and thus could illustrate the humanist ideal that all people share a universal soul. Since invisible man evokes the flamenco in the same sentence, he strengthens this notion. The first part of the image shows the universal truth that all humankind feels pain; in suffering all people are alike. But during the days of slavery, black people were categorically, legally, and socially denied their humanity. Therefore, the black subject must first of all be recognized as human.

If the humanist credo that all people are basically the same and of equal value can be seen on the first level, on the second we see that historical circumstances do and will erase such an idealism. The female slave who is pleading with the white slaveowners aptly demonstrates how differences of race, gender, and class prove stronger than the timeless humanist ideal. Difference erases sameness. Facts erase ideals. Body erases idea. Existence takes precedence over essence. The young black female slave has the same soul as the white slaveowners but, because her body is black and female, they can, in the interest of materialism, bargain over her body and reify her existence. Being both black and female, she is doubly oppressed. The second level of invisible man's cave image provides an eloquent critique of the humanist ideal and the universalism put forth on the first level of the cave.

The subjectivity the invisible man describes cannot, however, be limited to a discussion of nature and history or humanism and materialism. For him blackness is also a discourse, a textual system which is formed in the language of the slaveowners, but which must be rescued and redefined in terms which are also African American. On the third level of the cave image invisible man illustrates the doubleness of all terms which are used for cultural representation. On this level a black preacher is delivering a sermon on the blackness of blackness. Using the inherent African American technique of call and response, the preacher announces that his text this morning is the blackness of blackness and the audience responds that that blackness is most black.[6]   The call and response situation illustrates the sharp difference of all terms depending on their cultural context. The preacher here seems to act like a translator who takes a word from one context and gives it to his congregation who in turn gives it a new context. The hermeneutic quality of their dialogue illustrates the doubleness of cultural terms which have different meanings in different contexts and which become the sight for interpretation and power struggles. The striking postmodernist impression of *Invisible Man* partly stems from this acute awareness of the contingency of meaning and the importance of interpretation. If, as the congregation maintains, blackness is most black then the meaning of blackness must first of all be sought in its own context and not comparatively. When he states that there was blackness in the beginning, the preacher starts this search by evoking a state of blackness without doubleness, possibly alluding to a past in black

Africa. The congregation provides an ongoing commentary on the history of African Americans and of doubleness when they respond that black is bloody, black is red. This way they indicate that no definition of blackness can ignore its painful history or limit its nature by it. Thus the meaning of blackness must also be sought comparatively. Even if the meaning of blackness will always be established in its historical context, as a sign blackness too is subject to the reversibility of the sign. The preacher reflects this uncertainty as he goes on to preach a string of paradoxes: Black is and black "ain't." Black will get you and it "won't." Black will make you or black will unmake you. The preacher's unwillingness to determine the meaning of the sign serves as a reminder of its non-referential nature and the significance of doubleness which is the intense struggle for cultural meaning and survival.

This preacher also reminds the reader of one disturbing division of experience in Ellison's cave-image since the speaker is male. The cave image with its three levels has been archetypal in Western thought ever since Plato connected it to questions of essence, existence, and art.[7] Plato's image of the cave is also divided into three parts: the part where the prisoners are kept, the place where the fire is burning, and the outside where the sun is shining. The image evokes issues of appearance and reality, or substance and shadow. Connected to the underground image, it is also a useful image for the construction of subjectivity. But in invisible man's setting this grotto-scene, the cave-experience, the allegory of the fortunate fall in Western literature is not only archetypal but "arche-typical" as well, because it affirms the gender difference: Men have always built their voices while women of both races have remained mute and listened.

Possibly alluding to the way in which blackness has been associated with the devil in white Western discourse, invisible man brings up the three-tiered image again in the main part of the novel. When invisible man gets a job at Liberty Paints he is sent into the basement to become the assistant of Lucius Brockway. The basement is deep and three levels underground invisible man finds a door marked "Danger" where he enters. The room is noisy from the sounds of machines and it smells slightly of pinewood. This description of the descent into the underground through a door marked "Danger" with the smell of pinewood associated with fire and a man named Lucius (i.e., Lucifer) waiting at the bottom seems quite familiar. Since the image has been foregrounded in the Prologue, the doubleness of the cultural meaning is prepared. The associations to Plato's cave are also reinforced during the discussion invisible man has with his new boss, Brockway, about what is made in the basement. Invisible man has been led to believe that the paint is being made upstairs, but he soon learns that Brockway engineers the real paint in the basement and that upstairs the white workers only mix colors.   This situation exposes invisible man's readiness to believe that white men do the real job and it teaches him to question the appearances of images produced in the white culture. The allusions to the Platonic questioning of appearance and reality strengthen the irony of the doubleness. But invisible man not only repeats the three-tiered descent underground, he also signifies on the image when he reverses it in the Brotherhood chapter where invisible man gets an office on the third floor. Invisible man is probably never so deceived about appearances and reality as during his days with the Brotherhood. Therefore it seems significant that he reverses the image of a cave three levels deep with a building three stories high. If invisible man has found a substantial cultural truth at the bottom of the basement, he will find a substantial lie in the Brotherhood who swears allegiance to black people only to exploit and conveniently abandon them as they see fit.

The Dialogic and the Double Subject

There are strong links between the African American narrative of *Bildung* and the classical *Bildungsroman*. A text about the coming-of-age of a nameless young black protagonist, *Invisible Man* seemingly reproduces the structure and subjectivity of any *Bildungsroman* from Goethe's classic *Wilhelm Meister* onward. The long narrative story within the framing Prologue and Epilogue describes invisible man's maturation process in a linear and chronological fashion, thus reproducing the classical structure.

The main narrative also returns the sense of subjectivity inherent in the classical *Bildungsroman*. Invisible man starts out by calling himself naive and ends the story with a feeling that he has become whole, two self-descriptions which certainly reproduce the maturation process of the classical *Bildungsroman*. But there are major differences between the subject of the classical *Bildungsroman* and that of the African American narrative of *Bildung*. One of the most striking differences lies in the relationship between the subject and the surrounding society. The classical *Bildungsroman* celebrates the complete selfhood attained through the constant interaction between the internal unique self of the individual and the external communal self in society at large. The relationship between the individual and the society in the classical *Bildungsroman* may be seen as a kind of doubleness but, because the classical *Bildungsroman* is progressive and aims at canceling differences, this relationship is often structured in a dialectic way. In Goethe's novel, the protagonist Wilhelm Meister succeeds in elevating his status both on a personal and on a social level. The concluding synthesis in Goethe's novel illustrates the most celebrated theme of the classical *Bildungsroman*, that of compromise (Moretti 9). This compromise must also be regarded as the end of marginality and exile. It is instead an arrival, a homecoming, a return to family and society which ensures the reproduction of both. The concluding synthesis marks the end of the split, divided subject, and it indicates one of the main differences between the dialectic subject in the classical *Bildungsroman* and the double subject in the African American narrative of *Bildung* who can expect no such welcome into society as a final prize for maturity.

If one of the main thematic differences between the classical and the modern *Bildungsromane* is to be found in the relationship between the individual and his or her society, the framing of the text provides the main structural difference. Even though the frame tale is, in the words of Kerry McSweeney, "one of the staple conventions of prose fiction" (27), it illustrates a major shift of sensibility between the classical and the modern narratives of *Bildung*. To break the impact of the linear chronological structure of the classical *Bildungsroman* both Ellison and Dostoevsky frame their middle narrative sections with a Prologue and an Epilogue. (In *Notes from Underground* the section entitled "Underground" is equivalent to a prologue and the last three sentences in the novel constitute an epilogue.) The structural effect is twofold. First, the two framing parts bend the shape of the story into a circular structure. Simultaneously, they open up the structure at both ends by questioning both the notion of origin and that of *telos* implicit in the classical *Bildungsroman*. The framing parts of both *Notes from Underground* and *Invisible Man* suggest a critique of the positivistic and dialectic notion inherent in the linear progressive structure of the classical *Bildungsroman*. This structural device also adds a second or a double perspective on the subject, and it captivates the subject in a dialogue or a doubleness. This structural difference further highlights the other main difference between the classical and the modern *Bildungsroman* which is the double subject who both narrates the tale and is an agent within that tale. The third person voice that speaks of Wilhelm Meister neither compromises the subject nor is compromised by it. The distance between the narrating voice and the subject remains quite neutral, unaffected, and non-contagious. If the subject gets deadly ill, the narrator remains healthy. In the modern narratives of *Bildung*, however, this neutrality is abandoned. The double structure and the double subject of the modern narratives of *Bildung* exclude the very notion of a discourse which can remain objective and outside of the subject it discusses. The diseases it formulates, it also contracts. This ambiguous position informs the double discourse of the modern narratives of *Bildung* which are, to some degree, bound to reproduce on the page the things that they condemn. In this manner, the double subject further illuminates the complex and contradictory position of all oppressed people who in order to gain insight of their situation must reformulate the oppressive structures they want to escape. But in spite of these similarities, there are major differences between the white Western dialogic subject and the African American double subject. As we will see, the dialogics which Bakhtin so vividly describes are eternal and inescapable. But the doubleness of the African American subject represents a split which may also become a creative possibility for change in the subject position. Caught in the double position but not always content with it the African American double subject often seems to use the split to escape the endless dialogue of textuality. He or she produces a doubleness of world and text, history and story, which spells the end of the subject and refocuses the reader to the world. Undoubtedly, this position provides a critique of Western forms of cultural representation and the Western text.

There are several points of reference between the modernist and postmodernist narratives of *Bildung*. These reference points typically emphasize the general differences between the classical and the modern perspectives, such as, for example, the narrative point of view. In *Wilhelm Meister* the third person narrator remains not only outside of the events he (for it is a he) narrates but also on top of them. The point of view is from above. Controlling a lofty perspective over the complete chronology of Wilhelm Meister's life the narrator looks down at the events as if they were taking place on a stage below. In contrast, both the narrators and the protagonists of *Notes from Underground* and *Invisible Man* are literally and metaphorically underground. Yet, this similarity serves to emphasize the culturally different meanings of the underground image in the European and the African American traditions.[8] In Dostoevsky's novel the underground symbolizes the subject's social and psychological failure, his poverty, and personal isolation. The underground image represents the end of choices and alternatives; for the underground subject, it signifies closure.

In African American culture and history, however, the underground is a double sign, which marks both the end of slavery and a new beginning; it signifies both closure and rupture, both death and birth. Historically, the Underground Railroad was an organized institution which helped fugitive slaves from the southern plantations to freedom in the north. Originated probably as early as the eighteenth century, it grew into an institution during the nineteenth century. The distinguished historians John Hope Franklin and Alfred A. Moss, Jr., describe one plausible background to the naming of this institution when they suggest that the name Underground Railroad was probably coined after 1831 when the steam railroads became popular. They also suggest that the name may be connected to the story of one run away slave named Tice Davids who escaped from his Kentucky master across the Ohio river that same year. Franklin and Moss write that although "the master was in hot pursuit, he lost all trace of the slave after crossing the river, and was so confounded that he declared the slave must have 'gone off on an underground road'" (168). The secrecy surrounding the Underground Railroad has prevented an accurate estimation of how many slaves actually gained freedom this way, but Franklin and Moss follow the estimates of Governor Quitman of Mississippi who "stated that between 1810 and 1850 the South lost 100,000 slaves valued at more than $ 30 million" (172). The facts of the Underground Railroad may never be fully known, but the image of it has never ceased to fascinate the imagination and to grow in connotative significance. Loaded with tension and danger, it stands at the crossroads between slavery and freedom and in order to remain functional it demands silence and secrecy. Frederick Douglass for one describes his unwillingness to relate any facts about his own escape. "I have never approved of the very public manner in which some of our western friends have conducted what they call the *underground railroad*, but which I think, by their open declarations, has been made most emphatically the *upperground railroad*" (100). Born out of this silence, the image has produced some of the most eloquent passages in African American literature.

The image of the underground tends to reinforce the double position of the African American subject because it marks an oxymoron between enslavement and freedom as well as the suppression and the gaining of a voice. This doubleness is further emphasized because the double subject uses it both metaphorically and metonymically.[9] Sometimes it functions metaphorically to signify the intense desire for liberty and freedom from the destructive influence of the slave culture. Melvin Dixon argues that the underground, "the region in slave songs that lies 'down in the lonesome valley' where individual strength is tested and autonomy achieved, becomes, in modern texts, a stage for self-creating performances and for contact with black culture" (1987: 4). Other times, linking the geographical and social areas such as the North versus the South, Harlem versus lower Manhattan, the image of the underground used metonymically seems to reflect the very opposite of freedom. Both temporal and spatial, the underground image functions as a kind of Bakhtinian chronotope.[10] Even though Bakhtin's strict formal approach may appear alien to the African American tradition of criticism, the chronotope was one of Bakhtin's concepts that opened up the formal discourse to history.

Temporal and spatial, historic and utopian, the image of the underground becomes a main image for black *Bildung*. The African American literary tradition uses the image of the underground to describe what Jean Toomer calls "the root-life of a withered people."[11] In *Invisible Man*, in Richard Wright's story "The Man Who Lived Underground," and in "Kabnis," the concluding story of *Cane*, the underground image signifies both the lack of and the possible link to the history and tradition of black people.[12] Typically, when the image indicates the lack of contact with and knowledge of the cultural past of black people or the secret passageway to freedom, it functions as a metaphor. However, when it links the South and the North, it usually becomes metonymical.[13] Ellison uses the underground in both metaphorical and metonymic ways. On the one hand, he describes his underground home as a hole in the ground. In effect, he argues that his hole, which is a warm hole, is not a grave and that, even though he is invisible, he is not a ghost. Alluding to the folklore of Jack-the-bear, he makes it clear that he is more like a bear in hibernation or a spring chick waiting for the egg shell to break. He is at the beginning of a passage, not at the end. As a metaphor, the underground image in *Invisible Man* reflects both the secrecy and the promise of the Underground Railroad. But invisible man also portrays his underground home in metonymic ways. He describes how he, as an invisible man, has stopped paying bills and now gets his electricity for free. Invisible man remains quite convinced that the electric company called The Monopolated Light & Power knows that electricity disappears somewhere in Harlem, but he says, his hole is not inside Harlem but in a border area. As a metonymy, the underground image in *Invisible Man* illustrates the contiguity of invisible man's underground which marks the division between the white world of lower Manhattan and the black world of Harlem.   The use of the underground image in both metaphoric and metonymic ways reinforces the subject's doubleness.

The underground man also uses a double code of metonymy and metaphor to describe the basement where he lives, but the only realistic description of the underground in Dostoevsky's novel is very short.   The underground man mentions how he settled down at the outskirts of Petersburg in a room which is "dismal, squalid, at the very edge of town" (4).   In contrast he develops the metaphoric aspects of his existence into a virtual allegory where he becomes "the antithesis of the normal man" (10) and a mouse.   This mouse attempts to act like a man of action but, due to his doubts and questions, he does not succeed.   Instead, it pretends to be disgusted by the whole affair, to smile contemptuously at the world and hide itself in its hole.   Since it very well knows that this attitude is fake and that others in the world around it find it repulsive and ridiculous, it turns cold and malicious.

Both authors use metaphor and metonymy, but they stress them differently.   Dostoevsky develops the metaphorical sense of the underground into an allegory of social debasement.   Ellison, on the other hand, stresses the double nature of the underground image.   He uses the metonymic, contingent aspects of the underground to enhance the double position of the African American subject who must connect two cultures and who, like a passageway, links two worlds.   Invisible man's emphasis on the metonymic contributes to the doubleness of his discourse.   On the one hand, he develops the double nature of the African American narrative of *Bildung* while, on the other, he foregrounds the metonymic aspects of the underground image.   Since it has been suggested by Ihab Hassan among others that the metaphoric and the metonymic modes of writing distinguish modernism from postmodernism (1987: 91), this emphasis also contributes to the postmodernist impression in *Invisible Man*.

The use of the underground image in significantly different ways reflects how the two novels also share a similar yet different relationship to their readers, their real or imagined audience, and to other texts.   The African American narrative of *Bildung* infiltrates and reproduces the sick body of society in order to change and, hopefully, to provide a cure for it.

Exploring the ambiguity of closure, it attempts to influence the reader, to get out of the text, to turn its double discourse into a new reality. *Notes from Underground* in contrast contains a both pessimistic and fatalistic ritual of self-perpetuation; its most distinct feature—dialogism—illustrates well how it feeds on a sense of status quo. Mikhail Bakhtin writes that the most striking feature of *Notes from Underground* "is its extreme and acute dialogization: there is literally not a single monologically firm, undissociated word. From the very first sentence the hero's speech has already begun to cringe and break under the influence of the anticipated words of another, with whom the hero, from the very first step, enters into the most intense internal polemic" (1984: 227-228). The dialogic subject maintains a perpetual argument with an audience who is absent yet present in his dialogic monologue, but his attempts to reach out to others are feeble, and he remains most content when he can revel in himself. Invisible man in contrast reaches out and, eventually, interrupts his position as a narrative character. His narrative of *Bildung* is as determined by hidden discourses as is that of the underground man. The discourses absent-present in *Invisible Man* are primarily from two different traditions and they are treated in different ways.

Characteristically, invisible man "signifies on" the white tradition (Gates 1987: 246; 1988); he repeats, reverses, and parodies it. On the other hand, he tropes on African American literature. In order to establish an African American literary tradition and to build its recognition, he scrutinizes and re-evaluates works by black authors. There is, however, a difference between the dialogic discourse of *Notes from Underground* and the use of signifying in the double discourse in *Invisible Man*. The dialogic structure equalizes different voices while the signifying structure of *Invisible Man* reverses the hierarchy between the dominant white culture and the muted black culture. Shaping and celebrating its own tradition, the African American narrative of *Bildung* fosters a unique self-reflexivity within the African American narrative of *Bildung* and its double discourse, which are part of a conscious effort to change perception and interpretation of cultures.

This unique nature of the African American double discourse often disappears behind textual similarities which seemingly signal the identity between two texts such as, for example, *Notes from Underground* and *Invisible Man*. Formulating their own definitions of themselves and their societies, both the underground man and invisible man use the same opening strategy. Yet, as similar as these two opening passages are, they produce two distinctly different subjects. As subjects of modernity, both these subjects are double—they are both process and product—but even their doubleness shows how divergent they are because the African American double subject reflects the social illness in order to cure it, while the underground subject is proud of his disease and wants to maintain it. The underground man starts his story by saying that he is a sick man who does not know anything about his condition. He intimates that he is superstitious and that, even though he respects the medical community, he would not seek help there. It seems that his illness is an integral part of who he is and the one thing of which he feels most proud. To maintain his illness, he thinks that he does not need other people: he either excludes them altogether or he reduces them to a professional group of medical doctors whose services he slights. A modernist rebel guided by what Jürgen Habermas has described as "the principle of unlimited self-realization, the demand for authentic self-experience and the subjectivism of a hyper-stimulated sensitivity" (6), he seeks to evade other people's knowledge or ideas. Yet, quite contrary to his wishes, the dialogic discourse he creates is full of other people's opinions and ideas.

Invisible man also begins his story with a self-definition, but it is a definition loaded with his acute awareness of its relative and temporary nature. He does not claim ignorance and superstition like the underground man because he knows that it is ignorance and superstition in the people around him that causes his invisible condition. He has seen how they reduce him to his surroundings or use him to mirror their own hopes and fears. Invisible man also wants to create a special space for himself as a semiotic structure. To clarify that he will not reproduce an "already-read text" of blackness as a sign in a racist discourse, he distinguishes himself from Edgar Allan Poe's ghosts and Hollywood's ghostlike movie-characters. He also questions what Andreas Huyssen has termed the Great Divide between high art (Poe) and low art (Hollywood). Huyssen writes that postmodernism "rejects the theories and practices of the Great Divide" (viii). Invisible man's postmodernist refusal to partake in the quality distinctions serves as a critique of white Western categories which have been unsuitable for African American cultural products such as the blues and jazz, two art forms which certainly belong in both categories.

The two texts describe the development of two men who project very different notions of subjectivity and of *Bildung*. Both invisible man and the underground man attempt to define themselves by what they are and by what they are not, but the underground man is worried about being defined by a physical condition which, according to him, is marginal and unimportant. The malaise he wants to capture is mental, existential. Invisible man knows, however, that his "condition" is indeed physical—the color of his skin—but he also knows that the illness he describes is affecting the people around him; even if he is the only one aware of the illness, it is they who are sick.[14] His invisibility also seems to indicate that the problem goes much deeper and further than the differences of skin color. Both the underground man and invisible man discuss their respective situations in terms of illness but, unlike his underground brother, invisible man is looking for a cure. While the underground man maintains that it is "precisely their diseases that people pride themselves on" (5-6), invisible man argues that to passively accept one's condition is not enough; one must try to overcome it and proceed to new ambiguities and conflicts. His self-definition crystallizes against the history of objectified and reified slaves; ingeniously, he uses and reverses that status as he turns himself from object to subject. At the same time, the ambiguity of his opening statement is noticeable. When the underground man says that he is a sick man, his self-presentation is subject-oriented—somebody is sick in and of himself. But to be an invisible man is more object-oriented—somebody is invisible in the eyes of other people. The manner in which the two subjects construct themselves in relation to others and as individual minds indicates a major difference between them.

The way the dialogic and the double subjects relate to their illnesses is also reflected in how they perceive themselves as separate minds. The question of individual consciousness is crucial to both, but, because the dialogic subject is convinced that any consciousness is a disease, this too becomes an issue that separates them. In his comparison of the two novels, Joseph Frank describes *Notes from Underground* as "primarily a lengthy interior monologue of inner conflict, expressed in both ideological and psychological terms," not as a *Bildungsroman* capturing a process.[15] One reason for Frank's classification is the constant insistence on the part of the underground man that change is impossible. He believes that a man of consciousness, a man of intelligence, can no longer prosper in the modern world and so, even though consciousness is really all that he has, he resents it. His consciousness only makes him aware of his own degradation and strengthens his claustrophobia. He sees the situation of the modern man as a *cul-de-sac* where, even if he had enough time and faith to try to change, he could not do so because there is no longer anything to change into and no place to go. This pessimistic outlook leads the underground man to redefine himself not as a new kind of hero in a new kind of *Bildungsroman* but as an anti-hero subsumed by an earlier ideal.

Unlike the underground man, the invisible man cannot accept that his mind is a prison. When he sums up his underground situation at the end of the novel, he is still vibrating with the need and the desire for change. Even though he withdrew into a hole in the ground, it is becoming increasingly clear to him that his mind will not let him stay there. The dialogic subject argues with everybody and most of all with himself. He blames himself for his situation and becomes paralyzed by guilt-feelings. The double subject knows that he cannot accept the whole blame for his situation. At the end of the novel, he looks back at his story and realizes that he has been as invisible to some of the black people he has met as to the white people and he claims half of the blame for his situation. This division of guilt rescues him from psychological passivity and entrapment of self. Where the dialogic subject becomes increasingly re-individualized, the double subject uses the split in his or her position to escape self and becomes increasingly de-individualized.[16]

Invisible man's concluding desire for diversity and division (un)marks the conclusion by breaking it open. In the end invisible man argues that men are not solid and that their relationship are relative, that "men are different and that all life is divided and that only in division is there true health" (563). Even though this desire for diversity opposes the classical ideal of compromise, it shares in its didactic attitude toward its audience. Both the classical *Bildungsroman* and the African American narrative of *Bildung* project this dual purpose: the process of *Bildung* is directed as much toward the subject-protagonist as it is to the readers—the classical *Bildungsroman* because it expresses belief in the betterment of the individual human soul to the general improvement of humankind, an expression of positivism, and the African American narrative of *Bildung* because it wants to be a herald of change.

But how is change accomplished and who can carry it out? Arguing that there only are two alternatives, an essential or a decentered subject, many contemporary critics lament the empty space left after the disseminated subject in postmodernist fiction. Like Peter Currie they conclude that there is "certainly no 'transindividual collective subject' (Lucien Goldmann's phrase) . . . on the horizon ready to replace the negated subject of possessive individualism" (68). To my mind, this conclusion is based on the exclusion of the African American double subject. Invisible man's major contributions to the formulation of a postmodernist narrative of *Bildung* must be found primarily in the collective subject whose (hi)story is both personal and representational. Unlike the underground antihero, invisible man becomes what I like to call a "posthero." The African American history and heritage do not allow him to be content with a mere personal achievement. Unlike the classical Western hero, he cannot rely only on his own results. He not only investigates change but tries actively to instigate it and to produce the necessary force he needs to disappear out of focus. Therefore, he abdicates his privileged position as the narrator to become in the end a transparent voice, a free-floating signifier, indeed, an invisible x which, in a Brechtian manner, marks the shift of responsibility for change to us, his readers.

NOTES

1   *Invisible Man* has been called a *Bildungsroman* by, for example, Kenneth Burke. See also Earl H. Rovit, "Ralph Ellison and the Comic Tradition," *Wisconsin Studies in Contemporary Literature* 1 (1960): 34-42; Stewart Rodnon, "*The Adventures of Huckleberry Finn* and *Invisible Man*: Thematic and Structural Comparisons," *Black American Literature Forum* 4 (1970): 45-51, and Joseph Frank. See also Dietze 12-15.

2   Ralph Ellison discusses the writers he studied—Eliot, Joyce, Dostoevsky, Stein, Hemingway, and Malraux—in "The Art of Fiction: An Interview" in *Shadow and Act* (New York: Vintage, 1972) 167-183.

3   See, for example, Alan Nadel, *Invisible Criticism: Ralph Ellison and the American Canon* (Iowa City: U of Iowa P, 1988), Robert N. List, *Dedalus in Harlem: The Joyce-Ellison Connection* (Washington, DC: UP of America, Inc., 1982), and Rudolf F. Dietze.

4   Many African American critics argue that modernism took a different shape in African American literature. See, for example, Michael G. Cooke's *Afro-American Literature in the Twentieth Century: The Achievement of Intimacy* (New Haven: Yale UP, 1984). He writes that "While modernism in white literature took the form of hothouse virtuosity and detachment (if not revulsion) from the human, in Afro-American literature it took the form of a centering upon the possibilities of the human and an emergent sense of intimacy predicated on the human" (5). As critics go on debating the nature of postmodernism, they will surely formulate similar differences. See, for example, Robert Elliot Fox's *Conscientious Sorcerers: The Black Postmodernist Fiction of LeRoi Jones/Amiri Baraka, Ishmael Reed, and Samuel R. Delany* (New York: Greenwood P, 1987) and James W. Coleman, *Blackness and Modernism: The Literary Career of John Edgar Wideman* (Jackson: UP of Mississippi, 1989).

5   In African American literature one often finds the process of recognizing the past described as a movement in space.   This spatialized historiography suggests that the desire and the need to confront the past is equally strong for each new generation of African Americans. I discuss this issue further in the Conclusion of this book as well as in the article "Approaches to Africa: The Poetics of Memory and the Body in Two August Wilson Plays" *August Wilson: A Casebook*, The Modern American Dramatist Series. Ed. by Marilyn Elkins (Garland P, 1994). This use of space differs from postmodernist concerns about space both in architecture and literature as it has been explored by, for example, Fredric Jameson in "Postmodernism and Consumer Society."

6   For a discussion of the influence of the call-and-response structure of African American oral culture on black literature see John F. Callahan's *In the African-American Grain: The Pursuit of Voice in Twentieth-Century Black Fiction* (Urbana: U of Illinois P, 1988).

7   Part seven [book six] of *The Republic* is called "The Simile of the Cave" (London: Penguin Books, 1987) 316-325.

8   Joseph Frank comments that "It should be remarked that, in the 'underground railway,' the metaphor of the underground has an indigenous American meaning far richer than anything that can be found in nineteenth-century Russia, and Ralph Ellison did not have to read Dostoevsky to become aware of its symbolic resonances; but his reading of Dostoevsky no doubt gave him a heightened sense of its literary possibilities" (12).

9   For an in-depth discussion of metaphor and metonymy and how they function in African American literature, see chapter 3.

10   In *The Dialogic Imagination* Bakhtin writes that he "will give the name   chronotope   (literally,   "time   space")   to   the   intrinsic connectedness of temporal and spatial relationships that are artistically expressed in literature" Ed. by Michael Holquist, trans. by Caryl Emerson and Michael Holquist. (Austin: University of Texas Press, 1981) 84. See also the Conclusion.

11   See the short story "Box Seat" in Jean Toomer's *Cane* (New York: Liveright, 1975) 56.

12   For further exploration see Melvin Dixon's *Ride Out the Wilderness: Geography and Identity in Afro-American Fiction* (Urbana : U of Illinois P, 1987).

13   The distinction and opposition between the metaphorical and the metonymic types of writing was first developed by Roman Jakobson in the essay "Two Aspects of Aphasic Disturbances" in *Fundamentals of Language* (Leiden: Mouton's-Gravenhage: 1956) 55-82. See also Part Two of David Lodge, *The Modes of Modern Writing: Metaphor, Metonymy, and the Typology of Modern Literature* (Ithaca, NY: Cornell UP, 1977) and his "The Language of Modernist Fiction: Metaphor and Metonymy," *Modernism 1890-1930,* ed. Malcolm Bradbury and James McFarlane (London: Penguin, 1976) 481-496. See also the discussion by Robert Scholes, *Structuralism in Literature: An Introduction* (New Haven: Yale UP, 1974) 20-22. John R. Searle makes no formal distinction between metaphor and synecdochic metonymies, treating the latter as "special cases of metaphor." Yet, his chapter on "Metaphor" remains one of the best discussions on the topic available. See *Expression and Meaning: Studies in the Theory of Speech Acts* (Cambridge: Cambridge UP, 1979) 76-116. See also Kaja Silverman, *The Subject of Semiotics* (Oxford: Oxford UP, 1983) 109-122. I discuss this issue further in chapter 3.

14   In this invisible man reflects a long-standing tradition in black literature to comment upon the moral effects of slavery on white people.

15   Frank 13. Frank also argues that "*Invisible Man* is a negative *Bildungsroman,* in which the narrator-hero learns that everything he has been taught to believe by his various mentors is actually false and treacherous" (13).

16   In the Preface to *Anti-Oedipus*, Michel Foucault suggests that the "individual is the product of power. What is needed is to 'de-

individualize' by means of multiplication and displacement, diverse combinations.   The group must not be the organic bond uniting hierarchized individuals, but a constant generator of de-individualization" (xiv).

2

A Double Heritage: *Invisible Man*, *Wilhelm Meister* and *Narrative of the Life of Frederick Douglass*

> "How could this body have been
> produced by parents, when by its very nature
> it is such eloquent witness of its own self-
> production, of its own engendering of itself?"
>
> (*Anti-Oedipus*, 15)

> Every new artwork creates its own precursor.
>
> (Jorge Luis Borges)

"Anyone who analyzes black literature must do so as a comparatist, by definition, because our canonical texts have complex double formal antecedents, the Western and the black," Henry Louis Gates, argues in *The Signifying Monkey* (xxiv). In that scholarly study he also doubles his earlier definition of "signifying" to describe both the intertextual dialogue—or troping as he prefers to call it—within the African American literary tradition and the relationship of repetition and reversal between black literary texts and antecedent white Western texts. Making use of both these definitions of signifying, I hope to illustrate the complex relationship *Invisible Man* has to two of its literary antecedents, the slave narrative and the classical *Bildungsroman*. The slave narrative, exemplified here by Frederick Douglass' *Narrative of the Life* is a kind of African American narrative of *Bildung* focusing on, in the words of Douglass, "how a man was made a slave [and] how a slave was made a man" (68).[1] James Olney describes *Narrative of the Life* as "the greatest of the slave narratives and the most completely representative, embodying virtually every convention by which we can define and recognize the slave narrative" (3); therefore, I will use it here to exemplify the whole genre.

Generally, the slave narrative is a double story focusing both on the life of one man or woman while, at the same time, encoding the fate of all slaves. Though it draws a primarily individualistic portrait, the narrating "I" speaks from a collective experience.   The narrator of the classical *Bildungsroman*, on the other hand, poses as a *connoisseur* of reality and humankind in general, but he (for it is a he) tells a story of a singular and exemplary young man.   Whereas the slave narrative foregrounds the need for political and social changes,[2] the classical *Bildungsroman*, social and historical as it may be, depicts the personal maturation process of one unique individual.[3] Signifying on both traditions, Ellison's invisible man confronts their limitations and recodes the African American narrative of *Bildung* in order to disturb any placid notions of the "natural" process of maturation and the subject's "natural" position in the text.   The collision between these three narratives of *Bildung* illustrates not only the intertextual quality of Ellison's text, but also the various cultural codes shaping each story.   Illuminating the complex relationship *Invisible Man* has to its double literary heritage, the comparison focuses on the double aspects of the modern African American narrative of *Bildung* while highlighting the contingency of textual entities such as subjectivity, structure, and "the real."

In *S/Z* Roland Barthes often returns to the notion of a "Book of Life," a grand opus of "reality" as it becomes encoded in text. He argues that a "discourse has no responsibility vis-à-vis the real: in the most realistic novel, the referent has no 'reality'." In short, he continues, "what we call 'real' (in the theory of the realistic text) is never more than a code of representation (of signification): it is never a code of execution: *the novelistic real is not operable*" (80).   Even though the accumulated metonymical code of "the real" spells diversification and difference, Barthes seems to calmly assert that "we" share one "Book of Life." The comparison between three different narratives of *Bildung* crossing cultural and chronological borders shows, however, that it is exactly in the depiction of the real and the subject's interaction therewith that cultural difference becomes paramount.   Goethe's narrator woos the reader's complicity, assuming that the reality he depicts is not only well-known to the readers but also "operable." The didactic purpose in the classical *Bildungsroman* rests on the very basis that the story will improve the reader, encouraging him or her to follow the example of Wilhelm Meister. The thrust of the didactic purpose in *Narrative of the Life*, on the other hand, is ideological, political. It strives toward social and political changes in the realm of the real beyond the bettering of individual minds. The invisible subject, in contrast, involves the reader in a textual struggle; his didactic impulse becomes most noticeable in his attempts to recode the modern African American narrative of *Bildung*. Douglass' narrator and Goethe's narrator each assumes that his story replicates the life of a young man. The invisible narrator seems to want to make the real replicate his textual construction; he produces his text as a revolutionary act.

The dialectic relationship between subject and encoded reality also points to the main difference between the American and the European traditions of writing the narrative of *Bildung*. The classical European paradigm set by Goethe implies that chaos, anarchy, and rebellion spring from within the subject while a society, from without, implants order, rules, and stability. The general American literary tradition—of which the slave narrative is one outstanding example—reverses this distinction. Its main purpose is to uphold the innocence of the subject facing a cruel, unjust world. Invisible man goes a step further when he shows the reader how tenuous this very distinction is. His struggle convinces the reader that there is no "uncontaminated" inner space where the individual can keep his or her self intact or free from the world. But in spite of this poststructural dimension in the framing parts of the novel, the main chronological section of *Invisible Man* continues the distrust of organized society and its institutions common in both the white and the black American literary traditions.

The most striking parallel between the two African American texts, *Invisible Man* and *Narrative of the Life*, must be seen in the relationship between the narrator and his tale. Both these stories have a double function. They are told, presumably, for two reasons. First, drawn from what Roland Barthes in *S/Z* calls the Book of Life, each narrator encodes the life of a young black man in America. Second, both narrators want to

achieve mastery through the act of telling their tales. In other words, they
pursue similar goals both with the narrative processes and with the
processes of maturation the narrations encode. Both are narratives of
Bildung of sorts, and they also depict a double and "de-individualized"
process of maturation. In other words, each concentrates on how its
subject (that is the young subject Frederick—as a slave, as a fugitive, and
as a free narrating subject—and the invisible narrator-subject in *Invisible
Man*) learns that his life as a separate individual values little. Both authors
express that members of the black community often share a collective fate,
and that, consequently, history shapes their notions of a double and
contingent notion of selfhood.

In spite of this feeling of contingency, the second main feature linking
Frederick Douglass in *Narrative of the Life* and invisible man is a sense of
being apart, of being different. Douglass dwells on the difference between
slave children like himself who did not know their ages and white children
who could tell how old they were. Invisible man begins with a similar
distinction between, first, his text and white cultural products such as
Edgar Allan Poe's spooks and Hollywood-movie ectoplasms (3). He also
tells the story of how he fought with a white man who wouldn't apologize
for bumping into him. Invisible man almost kills the blond man before he
realizes that the man has not seen him, that he thought he was experiencing
a nightmare. While Douglass' *Narrative of the Life* focuses on the
difference between those who control and have access to the written,
historical record and those who, like himself, are left with the fallibility of
human memory, Ellison's *Invisible Man* opens with a recognition of the
difference between his and other sign-structures, and through context he
proceeds to link the different sign-structures to a discussion about people's
perceptions of reality. The incident with the white man becomes in the
newspaper a story about an aborted robbery, negating the experience of
invisible man. In order to adjust the impression given by the newspaper,
invisible man has to write his own version. By linking text and perception,
both Douglass' subject and the invisible subject emphasize the importance
of the textual, the written document whether historical or literary, in
shaping people's perception. In both, the lack of power over and access to

the written document illustrate the urgent need for their narratives of *Bildung* and the difference marking both.

The third person narrator of Goethe's *Wilhelm Meister* also feels a need to present Wilhelm Meister as different, but he does so mainly by setting him apart from the bourgeois setting of his immediate family, particularly his authoritative father. But the narrator also makes it clear that Wilhelm is different from the young actress he is pursuing at the opening of the novel. In dreaming of a future life as a theater director married to Mariane, young Wilhelm is mistaking both her and his own nature. Although she supposedly loves him, the actress is realistic and betrays him with an older, richer man. Through a web of details the narrator also reveals how Wilhelm's sense of order and beauty makes him unsuited for the sordid, unorganized daily life in the theater troupe. The three young protagonists are all different from people in their environments, but the way their difference is formulated shows how the three texts emphasize different aspects from the beginning. Invisible man concentrates on textual issues and the need to become visible. Douglass' subject tries to describe and analyze the effects of slavery. Even though the focus is on one particular individual, his written record is representational. Wilhelm Meister, on the other hand, is in conflict neither with other texts nor with a brutalizing institution such as slavery. His conflict is mainly with his father and his own mistaken wishes about his future. Whereas *Wilhelm Meister* is about a singular, unique individual, both *Narrative of the Life* and *Invisible Man* present the African American double subject that is, simultaneously, personal and representational.

Scholars and critics of African American fiction frequently call *Invisible Man* a *Bildungsroman*; rarely do they attempt to clarify what they mean by the label or the different ideological and literary assumptions contextualizing that term. Of all the critics applying the term, only Kenneth Burke develops the analogy between these two distinct traditions. In a published letter to Ellison, Burke notes some similarities between the lives of Goethe and Ellison and the protagonists they create. He sympathetically remarks that there "was the critical difference between Wilhelm Meister as white and your narrator as black. Whereas Goethe's father was quite well-to-do, you began with the vexations that were vestiges of life as experienced by slaves on the southern plantation" (354). Burke further discusses the three characteristic steps in the maturation process of Goethe's young hero—Apprenticeship, Journeymanship, Mastery—and he aligns these three phases with the maturation process of invisible man. He argues that "the character's step from apprenticeship to journeymanship is as clear as could be":

> His apprenticeship (his emergence out of childhood) concerns the stage of life when a black man at that time in our history was confronting strong remembrances from the days of the plantation from which "your kinds of humans" had not long ago by constitutional amendment been "emancipated." (351)

The second step, the journeymanship, takes place when invisible man goes to New York. Burke here remarks on the "ironically 'perfect' twist" (351) in Ellison's version of this stage of the narrative of *Bildung*, the *Wanderjahre*. In *Invisible Man* the young protagonist's grandfather has appeared to him in a dream earlier in the novel. In the dream the grandfather has a message, "Keep this Nigger Boy Running." This message ironically rewrites the European tradition of sending a young man on a cultivating trip through Europe in his youth. However, Burke's example is not the only ironic twist between *Wilhelm Meister* and *Invisible Man*. In both a general and a specific manner Ellison repeats and reverses Goethe's prototypical narrative of *Bildung*. In *Invisible Man* he shows that the ideal development projected in *Wilhelm Meister* is closed to anyone lacking Goethe's color and economic situation (and, one needs to add parenthetically, his gender). The third stage, the mastery, is quite clear in Goethe's case; as Burke points out, the goal of his maturation process is spelled out already in the name of the protagonist, Wilhelm Meister. However, in the case of *Invisible Man*, that stage remains ambiguous and unspecified, noticeable primarily in invisible man's mastery as narrator.

These three steps as gleaned from the maturation process of *Wilhelm Meister* help provide an overview of *Invisible Man* and the African

American narrative of *Bildung*. Yet, it is obvious that Goethe's work need not have inspired Ralph Ellison since these same basic steps are principal features of narrative scaffolding in the African American slave narrative which is a direct antecedent of the African American novel. *Narrative of the Life* is also structured as a text in three parts: apprenticeship, journeymanship, and mastery. However, there is a major difference in that Wilhelm Meister pursues a career within a sympathetic society, while the subject Frederick Douglass' period of apprenticeship primarily teaches him the degradations of slavery. In order for him to reach "mastery," he must first escape the American South and become a free man. Therefore, on a linear, syntagmatic level of narration there are more parallels between *Invisible Man* and *Wilhelm Meister*, both of which deal with young men who are not slaves. These similarities and differences further stress the necessity to illuminate the double heritage of the African American narrative of *Bildung*.

If one analyzes the classical *Bildungsroman* further by breaking it into more detailed, if equally schematic, parts, one finds that a curious pattern of repetition and reversal exists between it and *Invisible Man*, a pattern which justifies both the comparison and the rather simplified view it presents of both novels.[4] Syntagmatically, then, or in a linear and chronological fashion, one can identify six moments or steps within the development of the subject in the classical *Bildungsroman*, all six of which Ellison reproduces and reverses in *Invisible Man*. The classical *Bildungsroman* charts the rite of spring of a young man who journeys from immaturity and *naiveté* to maturity and *savoir-faire*. Under the term *Bildungsroman* Margaret Drabble describes the typical chain of events[5]:

[The] term applied to novels of education [dealing with] the innocent, inexperienced, well-meaning, but often foolish and erring, young man who sets out in life with either no aim in mind or the wrong one. By a series of false starts and mistakes and with the help from well-disposed friends he makes in the course of his experiences, he finally reaches maturity and finds his proper profession.

In her study *Social Mobility in the English Bildungsroman*, Patricia Alden supplies a fuller description of the genre:

> The genre focuses on the development of a single individual within a particular social world; it may be in part autobiographical; it is likely to give the history of this individual from childhood up to a point at which the development or unfolding of his or her character is achieved; in other words it is the story of apprenticeship rather than a life history. Central to the genre is the notion of individual selfhood achieved through growth and of social experience as an education which forms, and sometimes deforms, that self. The projected resolution of this process is some kind of adjustment to society. Wherever it appeared, the Bildungsroman was associated with bourgeois humanism, with faith in progress and with the value of the individual. (1)

The process of maturation captured in the classical *Bildungsroman* is that of a young man's combined development and cultivation until he becomes a mature and useful human being. As this process is illustrated by Goethe's *Wilhelm Meister*, it can be broken down into six steps, all of which can be recognized in *Invisible Man*. These six steps (twice the number Goethe and Burke identify) provide a basis for a fuller, more detailed comparison between the two novels. Approaching *Invisible Man* from this vantage will also remind the reader or critic how closely related the American Dream is to the classical narrative of *Bildung* in spite of the singular emphasis on materialistic success that is a crucial ingredient in the American myth. The six steps or features which are crucial to the classical narrative of *Bildung* are: (1) a protagonist grows up in a stable family unit in a specific social milieu which he is supposed to reproduce; (2) the pressure to reproduce these structures causes him to rebel against both family and society; (3) in rebelling, the subject moves away from both his family and his social circle and begins a period in his development during which he meets friends in the establishment and foes in the subculture; (4) in due time this new circumstance makes the protagonist realize the foolishness of his dreams and he opts for re-adjustment to his family's situation; (5) this in turn leads him to seek personal happiness and social success; (6) his readjustment also motivates him to continue the family and thus to reproduce the society he earlier rejected.

These six steps or features in the process of maturation identified in the life of Wilhelm Meister are all reproduced in *Invisible Man*, but they are repeated with a difference. Gates calls Ellison "the Great Signifier" (1987: 244). Indeed, there are many studies devoted to Ellison's ability to use, for his own purposes, African American and white Western concepts, tropes, and literary structures.[6] His double relationship to the African American narrative of *Bildung* and the classical *Bildungsroman* further exemplifies this technique. Briefly stated, Ellison's version of the six steps is as follows: (1) Invisible man has no family name and we learn next to nothing about his family. Whereas Wilhelm Meister rebels against his family and his society, (2) invisible man tries very hard to adjust to the dominant society and to become accepted by both the black and the white communities. During his process of maturation, (3) invisible man meets both white and black foes in the establishment and friends from the two races in the subculture. Instead of a period of adjustment to the demands around him, (4) invisible man suffers an accident in a paint factory and becomes an outcast. As a result of the dominant society's failure to recognize his abilities, (5) he becomes a professional and social failure who goes underground. This period ends with (6) a wish to finalize his hibernation and a demand for changes in the society. A close observation of how Ellison revises these six moments from the classical genre makes it clear how he uses the classical *Bildungsroman* as a hidden discourse which he forces into dialogue and thus further emphasizes the double heritage of invisible man's modern African American narrative of *Bildung*.[7]

Lessons in Doubleness

The earliest example of this double pattern of repetition and reversal can be seen in the names and titles of both protagonists and novels. Wilhelm Meister clearly inherits a name full of pressure and promise, but it is a name he is eventually able to live up to. His name is as descriptive as is that of invisible man. However, the African American tradition within which Ellison writes necessitates a different reading of invisible man's relative namelessness since the quest for a name separated from the institution of slavery dominates the African American tradition. For Douglass' subject the question of his name becomes urgent as soon as he reaches freedom. He describes how his name "given me by my mother was, 'Frederick Augustus Washington Bailey.' I, however, had dispensed with the two middle names long before I left Maryland so that I was generally known by the name of 'Frederick Bailey'" (109). His escape north necessitates a new name and so he asks one of his beneficiaries to give him a new last name. "I gave Mr. Johnson the privilege of choosing me a name, but told him he must not take from me the name of 'Frederick.' I must hold on to that, to preserve a sense of my identity" (110). In the African American tradition a person's name is often double, surrounded with the same associations as was the underground, discussed in chapter one. The name is a source both of secrecy and desire; it indicates both the lack of a past and the link to the past.

But the names in the African American tradition often also have a double function, linking the present to the future. The African American tradition of signifying uses names in a remarkable fashion to indicate an array of things about the character with that name. Trueblood, Bledsoe, Rinehart, Breedlove, Tar Baby, Milkman—the list of such names in African American fiction is long. One of the most significant of such names, however, is that of the nameless protagonist, invisible man. His name is both a description and a paradox: it establishes existence as it erases it. It stands for both presence and absence. Gates argues that "Ellison tropes with *Invisible Man*, invisibility an ironic response of absence to the would-be presence of 'blacks' and 'natives' . . . " (1987: 245). Once again we see how Ellison effectively plays on his double heritage, repeating and reversing a convention as he names his character after the typical condition of black characters by calling him invisible. At the same time, instead of remaining a marginal or invisible sign in a racist discourse, this invisible man claims the center and writes, visibly, his invisible self.

Invisible man's "name-less name" has a double function. On the one hand it distances him from the Book of the Real and makes the subject writerly. But, on the other hand, it shows the plight of a people who were violently uprooted from their homelands and brought to a foreign country where they were soon enslaved. Invisible man's lack of a family name illustrates the rupture of the Middle Passage. In contrast, the name Wilhelm Meister grounds that subject in a realistic and readerly tradition which is both positivistic and paternalistic. It includes the dream that a young son not only repeat his father's life but also make it better. But the conflict between father and son often begins with their different views on what actually will improve the family. Traditionally, the father upholds the values of materialistic success while the son wants to enlarge his inner abilities. This conflict can be seen at the beginning of *Wilhelm Meister* when Wilhelm's mother warns him of his father's displeasure over his interest in the theater. He impatiently asks her if everything is "useless which does not immediately put money in our pockets and which does not procure us possessions near at hand." In contrast, in the theater he is seeking "things which will entertain, enlighten and elevate us" (I:19). His goals exceed those of the immediate family and its material status. He longs to have an influence beyond "the narrow circle within which others wear themselves out with anxiety" (*WML*, I: 54).

The strong presence of the family circle is clearly reversed in *Invisible Man* where the immediate family is almost as elusive as the family name. All the reader learns about the invisible subject's ancestors is that his grandparents were slaves who one day were told that they were free and equal, yet separate like the fingers of the hand. Believing in this picture, his grandparents remained where they had always lived, kept working hard and raised his father to do the same. But even though the grandfather may have lived as if he believed in the doctrine of separate but equal existence in one (divided) nation, he refuses to die in that belief. He dies exposing the lie that cuts the smooth surface of the myth when he formulates the verbal will which begins the story of invisible man's maturation process.

When he is dying, invisible man's grandfather calls himself a traitor and a spy in the enemies' country and he tells his son to pretend to adjust and cooperate only to be better situated in order to destroy the white society one day. He advises his son "to overcome 'em with yeses, undermine 'em with grins, agree 'em to death and destruction, let 'em swoller you till they vomit or bust wide open" (16). With these words the grandfather dies, but paradoxically they also make him come alive because his words made everybody so upset that they could not forget him. This piece of advice and the anxiety it causes influence invisible man to seek acceptance from both the black and the white society. He has yet to understand the complexity of his double position.

Both invisible man and Wilhelm Meister are mistaken about their potentiality and possibilities. They set out with certain goals in mind which they cannot fulfill, but the deception works on different levels. In thinking that the theater is the proper channel for his abilities, Wilhelm Meister is deluding himself. Invisible man, however, is not only deceiving himself, he is also being deceived. When he goes to a meeting in order to deliver a speech in front of the leading white men in his town he thinks that they are the only people who can appreciate his talents. At this stage in his development he thinks that he is visible to them and that they will judge his performance properly. The youthful errors of the two protagonists are of a very different kind since Wilhelm Meister is mainly mistaken about his own nature; his mistake actually serves only to enlarge himself. The "mistake" of invisible man is that he thinks that he has a right to choose his own destiny apart from the culture around him, and that based on his own ability he can shape his future. His process of maturation shows him with cruel clarity that, in front of these and other white men, he is an invisible man. One major step during this process is to understand the importance of masking.

As I noted in the Introduction, one of the most potent descriptions of the duality of a black person's life is to be found in James Weldon Johnson's *The Autobiography of an Ex-Coloured Man*. As ex-coloured man describes the impact of his realization that he is black, he comments on "the dwarfing, warping, distorting influence which operates upon each and every coloured man in the United States.   He is forced to take his outlook on all things, not from the view-point of a citizen, or a man, or even a human being, but from the view-point of a *coloured* man" (403). He further describes the consequent duality of a black person in a white society:

> It is a difficult thing for a white man to learn what a coloured man really thinks; because, generally, with the latter an additional and different light must be brought to bear on what he thinks; and his thoughts are often influenced by considerations so delicate and subtle that it would be impossible for him to confess or explain them to one of the opposite race. This gives to every coloured man, in proportion to his intellectuality, a sort of dual personality; there is one phase of him which is disclosed only in the freemasonry of his own race. I have often watched with interest and sometimes with amazement even ignorant coloured men under cover of broad grins and minstrel antics maintain this dualism in the presence of white men. (403)

The complexity of this lesson indicates one of the major differences between the classical *Bildungsroman* and the African American narrative of *Bildung*. The African American subject, such as invisible man, must discover his or her doubleness and learn the difference between who he thinks and feels that he is and what a predominantly white society regards him as being. Wilhelm Meister's self-delusion and rebellion against his father's wishes illustrate his ardent wish and birthright to be himself, to be such as he imagines himself to be, to master his being. Forced to see himself also through the eyes of a hostile white community, invisible man must, in contrast, accept a double identity.

Invisible man's education in masking is rooted in his grandfather's verbal inheritance and trailed by its ambivalent doubleness. When he carries out his grandfather's advice he finds himself a tremendous social success and becomes a figurehead for both the black and the white communities, but while he is enjoying his success, he also feels a creeping unpleasant sense of guilt as if he has become a traitor to his people.

Invisible man's feelings toward his relationship to the white men indicate his inability at this stage to analyze the situation properly, as did, for example, ex-coloured man.   To invisible man a proper reading of his double personality becomes a major part of his process of maturation.

Invisible man needs to understand his relationship not only to the powerful white men in his hometown, but to his own and other people as well.   He tends to think that, not unlike Wilhelm Meister, he can have smooth   relationships   with   white   people,   relationships   that   are uncomplicated by issues of race and class and gender.   He believes that he has friends in the establishment and foes in the subculture, and it takes him many bitter moments to realize that every time he trusts somebody in the establishment, whether black or white, he is betrayed, and that it is among his often relatively powerless friends in the subculture that he can really learn something that will help him with, for example, his understanding of masking.   Attempting to attach himself to successful people, invisible man repeats Wilhelm Meister's behavior.   He soon discovers, however, that they are not what they seem and—in their eyes—he is not what he thought he was.   The African American narrative of *Bildung* always includes a painful recognition of the subject's lack of control over his or her own subjectivity.

The protagonist in the classical *Bildungsroman* also meets resistance to his ideas.   Wilhelm's father opposes his son, making him feel rebellious. Trying to avoid a major break with his family, Wilhelm Meister goes on a business trip for his father, but instead of concentrating solely on exploring and exploiting his father's business contacts, the young Wilhelm Meister stays with his friends in the theater company.   He even goes so far as to lend money to Molina, allowing the theater director to buy the equipment for the theater group, a stupid transaction since there is a great risk that Wilhelm will never see his money again, and even if he does, he earns no interest on it in the meantime.   Wilhelm Meister squanders both his time and his father's money in non-profitable ways during this period of time, but he also allows innate qualities to grow.   He will not leave this unprofitable life-style until he himself realizes that he should.   Even though he rebels against patriarchal power structures, the protagonist in the classical *Bildungsroman* remains untouched and supreme in his own being. He projects an image of a unique subject whose changes occur in a time and space continuum separated from the surrounding environment. Wilhelm Meister initiates and concludes both good and bad changes in his being.

Yet, the protagonist in the classical *Bildungsroman* never goes completely astray. Regardless of the stupid or dangerous things he does during his period of individual rebellion, he always meets influential strangers who help him when he is on the brink of catastrophe. Wilhelm Meister encounters several mysterious men who seem to know much about him and who give him good advice. Later he finds out that they all come from the Society of the Tower. The first mysterious stranger he encounters is a man who knows about his grandfather's art collection and who tries to convince him that fate does not exist. Man, if he wants to, is master over his life.

> The texture of this world is made up out of necessity and chance; man's higher reason comes between the two and can dominate them; it can guide, lead and make use of chance factors, and only when it stands firm and unshakeable, does man deserve to be called a god of the earth. Unhappy is he who from early years becomes accustomed to trying to find something arbitrary in what is necessary, who would like to attribute to chance elements a kind of higher reason, the following of which would in fact be a matter of religion. (I: 67)

In another instance, during the performance of *Hamlet* when Wilhelm fears that his production will fail and no ghost arrive, two "tall men in white cloaks and hoods . . . were standing in the wings" (II:105). Suddenly the Ghost appears, speaking with a voice which "seemed known to everybody, and Wilhelm believed he could notice a similarity with his father's voice" (II: 106). When the secret friend who played the Ghost disappears after the performance, he leaves behind a piece of cloth, a veil, with an imperative warning: "For the first and last time, take flight! Young man, take flight!" (II: 111). Young Wilhelm Meister's playful but

anarchic friends in the theater company try to lure him away from a more
prosperous career by encouraging him to stay and play with them, but
during that whole period of time, influential strangers follow Wilhelm to
make sure that he does not get really hurt in any way. Eventually, when
Wilhelm has lost both time and money, the Baron gives him a purse with
gold which makes it possible for him to contact his family without shame
since the gold covers his losses to Molina. The influence from these
strangers and Wilhelm's own experiences slowly convince him that his
dream about the theater life was illusory. But he will make no changes in
his pursuits until he himself is convinced thereof.

Having to come to terms with the double African American subject
position, invisible man's maturation process is more precarious. He has to
understand that the people in the establishment such as the Bledsoes and the
Nortons are not trustworthy, and that people like Trueblood and the Vet
whom he regards with suspicion are actually trying to help him. They
attempt to teach him crucial things about himself, his culture, his race, and
his situation. All these friends are people who, for one reason or another,
have failed to reproduce the steps of a successful *Bildung*. The first
friendly voice is the most influential, partly because it comes from his
grandfather, partly because of the startling circumstances when the old man
dies, and partly because his is the first indication of the puzzle that
invisible man attempts to solve. The grandfather provides an analysis of
race relations which, in due time, allows invisible man to see through the
myth of equal but separate like the fingers on the hand. Characteristically,
the great modernist novels have been variations on the detective novel.
Adding to the postmodernist dimensions of the novel, the shattering results
of slavery described in *Invisible Man* remain a challenging reality.

Invisible man's inability to distinguish between friend and foe is one
major consequence of the confusion caused by the double African
American subject position. For example, when he meets Trueblood, he
tries to distance himself from the illiterate sharecropper who has made his
own daughter pregnant. Trueblood gives invisible man two important
clues about the value of personal identity and racial, communal belonging.
First, in a clear reversal of Mr. Norton's view that people are getting

increasingly degenerate, Trueblood tells invisible man to be proud of his race and that black people are becoming better-looking. He also teaches invisible man an important lesson in survival—how to deal with insufferable pain. He narrates the long story about how he got his daughter pregnant, how he survived his daughter's and his wife's reactions, and how, eventually, he himself came to terms with his crime. He describes a series of useless attempts he made to deal with his act, including talking to a preacher, praying, and thinking until one night when he was looking at the stars he began to sing the blues.[8] The principal lesson Trueblood teaches invisible man is about the value and function of the blues which has helped and continues to help black people deal with intolerable suffering, with intolerable lives and deaths. The pain invisible man will feel may be his own, but as Trueblood reveals, people have learned how to live in spite of pain and they have shared this knowledge. Trueblood gives invisible man an early lesson in dealing with the double African American subject position.

The next lesson in survival and doubleness for invisible man comes from the crazy vet he meets on his bus trip to New York. With a Nietzschean sense of humor and way of thinking, the vet tells invisible man that "there's always an element of crime in freedom" (153). He also tries to encourage invisible man to stop believing in authority figures. He tells him to be his own father. Invisible man, who is carrying damning letters of recommendation does not yet know how apt this piece of advice is. In contrast to the protagonist in the classical *Bildungsroman*, invisible man has no substitute fathers in the establishment. Every time he trusts one of them he is betrayed until he learns to live as a double subject.

The protagonist as a victim of betrayal becomes even more obvious in New York City when invisible man goes from place to place with his condemning letters seeking work until he gets help from an unexpected quarter, the son of Mr. Emerson. A frequent patron of the night club Calamus, young Emerson knows and attempts to show invisible man how oppressive the myth of *Bildung* can be if one is excluded from it. In veiled language and half sentences, young Emerson tries to convey his knowledge to invisible man, who still believes not only in the altruism of the Bledsoes and the Nortons but also in his own ability and social possibility to reproduce the traditional narrative of *Bildung*. He still believes that as long as he wears the "right" clothes, exudes the "right" smell, eats the "right" things and behaves in the expected manner, good things will come to him. He tells young Emerson that he can "prove his identity" but Emerson no longer believes in the notion of identity and gives him Bledsoe's letter to read. In language befitting a Goethe imitator, Bledsoe has written a letter which condemns the carrier. Finally, invisible man recognizes the deception in the people he has been taught to trust. Once he grasps his position, he grows up fast as the insight affects all his memories.

Faced with this betrayal, the cruelty of which is that it destroys retroactively some of invisible man's fondest memories, the question of who he is becomes even more crucial. Left on his own, trying to take command of his own life, he seems to have lost any sense of identity. No longer trusting in any authority figures, he calls the Liberty Paints plant and gets a job. By gaining initiative over his own life invisible man reaches a level of self-confidence which Wilhelm Meister had from the start. However, the accident at Liberty Paints and the so-called medical treatment he receives following the accident demonstrate how illusory invisible man's personal power is. To be one's own father in a society which denies the rights of the individual proves impossible. Still weak following his operation, he is released from the Factory Hospital and he has little money to sustain him. He is nursed back to health by Mary Rambo, a black woman who adheres to values different from those of people in her environment. Expounding her value system and insisting that he do something that is a credit to the race, Mary tries to teach invisible man another lesson about the double African American subject, about individual pursuits, and communal belonging. She believes that it is only the black people from the South, the ones who still remember the pain from the fire as she puts it, who must transform the society. She thinks that many of the northern blacks have found a place for themselves and forgotten their less fortunate brothers and sisters. The way she sees it, she is in New York, but New York is not in her. In encouraging invisible man to become a credit to his race Mary repeats a common theme in the African

American literary tradition. Douglass, for example, describes how in secrecy he held a Sabbath school to teach his fellow slaves.

> These dear souls came not to Sabbath school because it was popular to do so, nor did I teach them because it was reputable to be thus engaged. Every moment they spent in that school, they were liable to be taken up, and given thirty-nine lashes. They came because they wished to learn. Their minds had been starved by their cruel masters. They had been shut up in mental darkness. I taught them, because it was the delight of my soul to be doing something that looked like bettering the condition of my race. (82-83)

The slave narratives, the classical *Bildungsroman*, and the modern narratives of *Bildung* share this desire to better the conditions of people, but the difference in general circumstances must be noted. In the African American tradition any constructive attempt to improve the conditions of the race is always perilous and pursued under severe restrictions demanding deception and masking, demanding a double life. The African American response to these restrictions from the dominant society is double. It creates the secrecy and desire surrounding the trope of improving the conditions of the race repeated and signified on in the African American literary tradition. It also creates the recurring tension between the desire for personal and communal improvement.

When he reads Bledsoe's letter, invisible man claims that hereafter he will never be the same person. But the real turning point occurs when, helped by Mary and the street yam vender, he returns to his roots and recognizes his double identity. Whereas Wilhelm Meister improves on his family by marrying into a class above his own, invisible man finds that only if he returns to his own community and culture can he avoid false father figures (black and white) and begin writing his own narrative of *Bildung*, a story which will be both personal and representational. The taste of buttery yams on a winter cold street in New York City motivates invisible man to voice his own rebellious motto: "I yam what I am." He has spanned a wide metaphorical circle back home and is now prepared to renew his search for his own, divided subjectivity.

Once invisible man ceases to deny his double identity, he finds not only a new sense of freedom but also his old ability to use words. This ability with words once took him away from his community, where he knew everybody's life, background, and religion to the anonymity and alienation of the city. Returning to his community in soul and mind if not in physical reality allows him a new sense of selfhood. In this new mental state he is able to shape from what he has learned and what he now sees as a new vision of his future. Walking down the street he stumbles onto the scene of an old couple being evicted from their apartment. Full of his new sense of identity he isolates himself from the crowd until he realizes that what is happening to the old couple also is happening to him. Their fate is a challenge to his isolation and his persistent feeling of shame at what he is witnessing. As invisible man slowly changes from passive spectator to active agitator, his sense of self changes from the personal "I" to a collective "we." The old household objects in the snow also make him remember things he has suppressed, and through the use of metaphor this act of remembrance is closely linked to the act of speech. The pressure of the invisible subject's suppressed memories reinforces the difference between human memory and written record. He begins to listen to a stuttering voice which offers a second challenge to the insular sense of subjectivity he has championed up to this point. This voice is both personal and communal; the new goal for invisible man is to let it speak with confidence and in daylight. He will eventually become that voice which formulates the African American double subject. But first he must find out what kind of voice it is and what the double subjectivity has in store for him. The remainder of the book dealing with invisible man's courtship and eventual rejection of the Brotherhood presents three alternative ways of being, seeing, and signifying self, all of which he tries and rejects before he begins to formulate his own self, to write his own subjectivity. These three alternatives are demonstrated in the lives of Jack and Ras in the first instance, Clifton in the second, and Rinehart in the third.

As different as they are, Jack and Ras are both fanatics who believe more in what they find in ideas than in what they see in reality. When

reality does not live up to their ideas, both resort to violence in an attempt
to force reality to fit their ideas. They talk a lot about the community in an
abstract way, but they don't listen to anybody, and their lack of caring
becomes increasingly evident during the riot. Shocked at the degree of
violence and disturbance, invisible man eventually decides that it is better
to live than to die for somebody else's ideas be it Ras' or Jack's.

In his own way Clifton, on the other hand, represents a subjectivity
closer to that found in Goethe's novel. He is the "exemplary," the born
leader of his people, the "black prince," and it is the greatest tragedy in
Invisible Man that he finds nothing to do with this self but to mock it with
racist Sambo dolls and, eventually, to provoke a cop to kill him—an act
close to suicide. With his death Ellison shows how little value individual
qualities have. Whereas Wilhelm's personal qualities enable him to
improve his personal life and that of his future family, Clifton finds no
constructive use of his mental and physical superiority. Everybody Clifton
meets recognizes that he has the qualities to outdo the Jacks and the Ras,
but even "a natural prince" is helpless as a singular individual (363). In
the Book of the Real depicted in *Invisible Man* the only single individual to
prosper is the one who is not singular, the one who masters many faces,
the protean Rinehart. Rinehart is, of course, the very opposite of Clifton;
he is the natural confidence man whose rind and heart cannot be separated.
Rinehart is the ultimate example of a postmodernist subject in the novel.
Invisible man approaches all three alternatives, but neither holds any
permanent attraction for him, because in spite of the appearance of
togetherness, brotherhood, and communality, all four men are aggressively
individualistic and, in their own ways, terribly narcissistic.

Neither Jack, Ras, Clifton nor Rinehart can provide invisible man with
the contingent subjectivity which he aspires to find. This collective sense
of self is a trace from the residually oral culture.[9] It is also an inheritance
from the slave narrative tradition. During slavery families were regularly
forced apart, but the slaves often forged new bonds with each other, bonds
as strong as many a familial bond. *Narrative of the Life* begins with a
statement about the individual subject: "I was born in Tuckahoe, near
Hillsborough, and about twelve miles from Easton, in Talbot country,

Maryland. I have no accurate knowledge of my age, never having seen any authentic record containing it" (1). But the focus quickly switches from the particular individual to the collective experience of all slaves. "By far the largest part of the slaves know as little of their ages as horses know of theirs, and it is the wish of most masters within my knowledge to keep their slaves thus ignorant" (1). Every experience he recounts he shares with other slaves. He tells of how he and his mother were separated—"before I knew her as my mother. It is a common custom, in the part of Maryland from which I ran away, to part children from their mothers at a very early age" (2). Douglass opens the story of his life with facts about his birth and infancy, but every instance of personal history shades into the collective history all slaves from that area share.

This collective sense of subjectivity increases rather than diminishes in *Narrative of the Life*. The last year before he becomes a free man, Douglass spends with a Mr. Freeland. During this year he plans and eventually executes his escape, but his wish to become free is inclusive, representational rather than individualistic. Whereas Wilhelm Meister pursues progression for himself and only through himself that of society, Douglass consistently includes his fellow slaves. "We were linked and interlinked with each other," he explains.

> I believe we would have died for each other. We never undertook to do any thing, of any importance, without a mutual consultation. We never moved separately. We were one; and as much so by our tempers and dispositions, as by the mutual hardships to which we were necessarily subjected by our condition as slaves. (83)

But slavery alone cannot explain the contingent subjectivity Douglass describes. He emphasizes that the collectivity nourished in African American culture also originates in the "tempers and dispositions" of black people; beyond the particular social and historical circumstances, it signifies the black difference.

Even though Wilhelm Meister's sense of subjectivity is comparatively singular, naturally he too is influenced by the people he meets. After a period of individual rebellion when he is drawn both to friends in the establishment and foes in the subculture, he enters a fourth moment when he begins to adjust to his society and the demands of his family. Traveling to Lothario's castle, Wilhelm Meister begins this stage when he decides to leave the theater after Aurelia's death. When Jarno asks him about the theater and whether he stayed long with the group, Wilhelm answers, "Longer than reasonable; for unfortunately when I think back to the time that I spent with them, I feel that I am looking into a void; I have retained nothing of this time" (III:7). True to his nature, Jarno of course argues with him:

'You are mistaken; everything that happens to us leaves some traces, everything imperceptibly contributes to our development; but it is dangerous to try to account for this ourselves. In the process we either become arrogant and lackadaisical or else downcast and faint-hearted, and both are destructive as regards the future. The safest thing always is to pursue only what is nearest and within grasp . . .' (III: 7-8)

The classical *Bildungsroman* questions the individual's ability to write his or her own story. As Jarno points out, the individual perspective is too limited and fallible to produce the proper perspective. Logically, the classical *Bildungsroman* is written in the third person. Such a belief in the individual's ability to construct his or her own subjectivity in writing is, however, strong within the African American literary tradition and constitutes one of the most important differences between *Wilhelm Meister*, on the one hand, and *Narrative of the Life* and *Invisible Man*, on the other. The suspicion directed against writing in the classical *Bildungsroman* may reflect a whole culture's fear of textuality. Ever since Plato threw out the poets from the Republic, the white Western tradition has been dominated by such a fear of the uncontrollable element of the written text. This culture identifies control, presence, identity, and oneness with the presence and subjectivity of speech. The double African American subject, however, relishes in the uncertainty of the written code, which gives him or her power and freedom to reverse many of the dominant definitions and hierarchies.

Belief in the process of writing one's own subjectivity marks a major difference between the African American texts and the antecedent Western text. However, so does the conclusions of that process. The fifth moment of the syntagmatic break-down of the classical *Bildungsroman* describes Wilhelm Meister's concluding happiness and social success. Once the young man has understood that he should channel his talents in a socially respectable direction, society stands ready to reward him by accepting him fully into its realm and giving him power and profits. The Society of the Tower has followed, guided, and warned Wilhelm throughout his tumultuous years. When he is ready to join them, they are equally ready to receive him and to give him all the ultimate answers. Though Wilhelm has trusted his own intuition in everything, he dares not do so in relation to his own son. Not until the Society assures him that his son Felix is actually his does he accept the responsibilities of a father. With these new responsibilities comes a new feeling of belonging:

> He no longer looked at the world as does a bird of passage, he no longer considered a building to be a summer-house that has been quickly put together and which dries out before it is left again. Everything that he was thinking of investing was to increase for the boy's sake, and everything that he set up was to last for several generations. In this sense his years of apprenticeship were over, and with a feeling of paternity he had also acquired all the virtues of a citizen. He sensed this, and his joy was incomparable. (III: 72)

This moment of return to the dream and reality of his father in turn leads to the sixth and last moment of the narrative of *Bildung* when the young man settles down. The end of his youthful rebellion leads to a prosperous marriage, to hope for future continuation of the family and the family name as well as to a reproduction of society. The identification between self and world is complete.

During a period which for Wilhelm Meister led to personal happiness as well as to indications of a prosperous social future, invisible man studies and discards the three alternative subjectivities he encounters through Jack, Clifton, and Rinehart. But this period must be described as one of social failure. His working for the Brotherhood under an assigned name cannot exactly be considered an example of professional success. The examples of his indulgence in parties and the overnight sexual affairs with women closely related to influential men in the Brotherhood uphold no strong evidence of his social success in either the black or the white community. Whereas Wilhelm Meister ends up reproducing and improving society, invisible man begins to review his sense of subjectivity, to formulate his own African American narrative of *Bildung*, and he demands changes in society.

Step by step, then, on a syntagmatic level *Invisible Man* reverses the narrative of *Wilhelm Meister*. These reversals, on the other hand, often provide links to Douglass' *Narrative of the Life*. Ellison's double formulation of the narrative of *Bildung* signifies on both the traditional slave narrative and on the classical *Bildungsroman*. The strongest reversal as it is reflected in the six steps just discussed is that of the relationship between the individual and his fate. At the outset of his maturation process, Wilhelm believes in fate; among other things his maturation process involves a change from disbelief to belief in his own powers to influence people and events. By the end, he is no longer a victim of fate; as father and husband, he controls his world. By allowing his natural talents to develop freely, he has become a complete human being who believes that his unique individuality is universal; Wilhelm Meister becomes the world citizen. Invisible man inherits this humanist belief in universality. At the outset of his narrative of *Bildung*, he believes in his right and his ability to shape his own life, to develop his innate talents, and in effect to repeat the life of Wilhelm. He, too, wants to become the world citizen and he hopes to arrive there through the Brotherhood, because he believes that it offers him a complete vision of how the world, its business, its hierarchies, operate. He thinks it offers him a way of looking at himself that transcends race, and if he only commits himself he can become a part of that world.

Of course, the remainder of his career within the Brotherhood demonstrates how wrong he is. Neither the Brotherhood nor the country nor the world is willing or able to reproduce these lofty Goethean ideals. The kind of subjectivity invisible man eventually recognizes, and which belongs to the African American tradition, is double. The African American subject comes to realize that alone he has no ability to influence the power structures in his society. In order to shape the world, he or she must recognize his double identity. Invisible man's slow discovery of his African American heritage, his understanding of masking, his attempts to formulate a double subjectivity as well as his consistent reveling in textuality and signifying, illustrate the double nature of the African American narrative of *Bildung*.

NOTES

1   Valerie Smith compares the slave narratives by Olaudah Equiano and Frederick Douglass to the classical *Bildungsroman*: "As the examples of Equiano and Douglass reveal, the representative hero of the slave narrative, like the archetypal hero of the *Bildungsroman*, moves from the idyllic life of childhood ignorance in the country into a metaphoric wilderness, in this case the recognition of his status as a slave" (33).

2   Blyden Jackson emphasizes the "drastic change" of one dominant function of the slave narrative by 1840: with Douglass' *Narrative*, it became openly abolitionist (110).

3   For a discussion of the historical and social frames in *Wilhelm Meister*, see Beddow.

4   Gates makes a similar comparison between Douglass' *Narrative of the Life* and the picaresque tradition as it was broken down into seven "characteristics" by Claudio Guillen (1987: 81-82). See also J. Lee Greene's article "The Pain and the Beauty: The South, the Black Writer, and Conventions of the Picaresque," *The American South: Portrait of a Culture*, ed. Louis D. Rubin, Jr. (Baton Rouge: Louisiana State UP, 1980) 264-288.

5   In *The Oxford Companion to English Literature* (Oxford: Oxford UP, 1985).

6   For a list of studies on the intertextual qualities in *Invisible Man*, see chapter one, notes 2-3.

7   For a discussion of Mikhail Bakhtin's concept of dialogization and its function in *Invisible Man*, see chapter one.

8   For an article on the role the blues plays in the healing processes among black women in novels by Toni Morrison, Alice Walker, Gayl Jones, and Toni Cade Bambara see my "The Blues, Healing, and Cultural Representation in Contemporary African American Women's Literature," *Women Physicians and Healers: Climbing a Long Hill*, ed. Lilian R. Furst (Lexington: Kentucky UP, 1997) 114-127.

9   Bernard Bell argues that "In contrast to literate cultures, residually oral cultures are basically aural, functional, collective, and direct. Like oral cultures, they stress performance, mnemonics, and improvisational skills. The tendency is to focus on the here and now, to employ some kind of formulaic mode of expression, and to subordinate the individual to the group or type" (20-21).

3

A Double Code: Language and the Female Subject in Toni Morrison's *The Bluest Eye* and Gayl Jones' *Eva's Man*

> "Otis said it was like they were
> working some kind of blues ritual.
> He said he couldn't stop watching."
> (*Eva's Man* 131)

> "feminine sexuality is not subject to metonymy"
> (Jane Gallop in *The Daughter's Seduction*)

In search of a subjective voice, the female African American narratives of *Bildung* often provide the sharpest examples of the tension between individual and community, history and language, experience and expression, body and word. In European and American feminism the effort to find a subjective voice through the female body has been intense, and it has often revealed that the cultural taboos surrounding such an enterprise are strong enough to render that voice almost mad. Who dares to speak like God? asks Hélène Cixous as she ponders her position as "Jewoman."[1] Such efforts to seek a voice through the body take on added vibrations in African American literature. In some cases the writing of and through the female black body in some cases must include stories of violent physical abuse and must show the abandonment of that body by a female community whose strategies for strength and survival it has challenged. Toni Morrison's *The Bluest Eye* (1970) and Gayl Jones' *Eva's Man* (1976) are two African American female narratives of *Bildung* which explore extreme and painful connections between the violated female body and the search for a female subjective voice. They also show that, within the black community as well as in society at large, the cultural taboos against the search for a black female subjective voice are strong enough to create a provocative combination of silence and madness which demands a new "literacy," a new way of reading the silence and anger of the abused body and the hysteria of the suppressed and contorted voice it creates. These novels illustrate the complex situation of the black female subject who, through violence and violation, loses her place in her community and is abandoned by it. In a lonesome and isolated search for her own words to capture her experiences, she seemingly loses her ability of rational communication, but much like the (s)hero of ancient fairytales and epic poems, she may also point to a new direction for the whole community. The collective nature of these experiences is further illustrated through the intimate juxtaposition of a bad society and a mad language; the interrelatedness between the *langue* of society and the *parole* of the individual suggests that, if incorporated, the perspective of these abandoned voices could transform and strengthen the whole community.

The Bluest Eye and *Eva's Man* are novels about silent girls who invent a language with which they can begin to speak or write themselves but, since their ways of communicating seem mad, their accomplishments are easily overlooked or belittled. This is especially true in the case of Pecola. In contrast to Eva's long and rambling confessional, the reader gets only a short glimpse of the subjectivity Pecola has created near the end of the novel in the dialogue Pecola spins with her invented friend. But this short glimpse does provide an idea of the nature of Pecola's madness and the language she has found. Against cultural and social expectations, both characters struggle to invent a language in which they are positioned as subjects, not merely as objects or victims of racial and sexual oppression. In so doing, they might sound mad, but the linguistic code they use is both rational and predictable. Theirs is a language of memory and desire often expressed through metaphor which they oppose to a code of racial and sexual abuse which they construct in metonymies. The title of Morrison's novel signals this doubleness of codes since *The Bluest Eye* is a metonymic title which evokes an audible double "The Bluest I" which is metaphoric. The importance of the communal and shared history of black women for the metaphoric code also shows how distant the European American paradigm of *Bildung* is in relation to the female African American narrative of *Bildung*.

The distinction between metaphor and metonymy is a quite recent phenomenon. Traditionally, a metonymy was considered a sub-group of metaphor, a different kind of metaphor maybe, but a metaphor nonetheless. The influential linguist Roman Jakobson changed that when he concluded that the metonymic and the metaphoric codes were not only different but opposed.[2] David Lodge explains Jakobson's conclusions.

> Rhetoricians and critics from Aristotle to the present day have generally regarded metonymy and synecdoche as forms or subspecies of metaphor, and it is easy to see why. Superficially they seem to be the same sort of thing—figurative transformations of literal statements. . . . Jakobson, however, . . . argues that metaphor and metonymy are *opposed*, because generated according to opposite principles.
>
> Metaphor, as we have seen, belongs to the selection axis of language; metonymy and synecdoche belong to the combination axis of language. (75-76)

For the purposes of this chapter I will define metonymy very narrowly as a *synecdochic* figure, a *pars pro toto*, in which a part stands for the whole. A metonymy, such as saying "I see three sails on the horizon" instead of saying "I see three ships," presupposes a real relation in the world between whole and part, between ship and sail. The metonymic figure projects features on a pre-existent chain from one end of the link to the other; the part is invested with all the features of the whole. With a metaphor, in contrast, no intrinsic relation in the world exists between the two parts of the link. In the metaphor "Achilles is a lion," there is no natural or worldly relation between Achilles and the lion. Whereas a metonymy involves a projection of features from one end of the link to the other, a metaphor involves an exchange of features via a third party. The metaphor only works when the image is familiar. If the reader does not know that the lion is brave, he or she would not understand the meaning of the metaphor. In a general sense, a metonymy suppresses difference and involves a relation of power and appropriation while a metaphor is a figure of difference on equal and culturally shared footing; it never involves relations of power between two entities. The differences between the rhetorical modes of representation are, however, also curbed by the fact that they both inscribe reality and defamiliarize it at the same time.[3]

Discussions about metaphor and metonymy abound in recent studies on fictionality and subjectivity. In "White Mythology: Metaphor in the Text of Philosophy" Jacques Derrida calls a metaphor "the trope of resemblance." He argues that it is "a metaphor that implies a *continuist presupposition*: the history of a metaphor appears essentially not as a displacement with breaks, as reinscription in a heterogeneous system, mutations, separations without origin, but rather as a progressive erosion, a regular semantic loss, an uninterrupted exhausting of the primitive meaning: an empirical abstraction without extraction from its own native soil" (215). Derrida's sense of a historical link, of what he calls a "semantic 'depth'" well matches what I will describe as a metaphoric chain. Alice A. Jardine ties the very definition of what she calls "gynesis," that is "the process of internalizing these [newly contoured fictional spaces, hypothetical and unmeasurable, spaces freely coded as] feminine spaces," to metaphor and metonymy. She describes the figurative modes somewhat differently as she sees in metaphor "the possibilities for difference and resemblance" and in metonymy "the possibilities for continuity and desire" (69). Since the subjectivity in these novels remains deferred and even utopian, it is also relevant to note with Kaja Silverman that sometimes both metaphor and metonymy "are used by literary and cinematic texts to sustain the absence of a given term indefinitely" or "to create a dialectic of absence and presence" (113). This flickering pattern between absence and presence well describes the position of the subject-under-writing in *Eva's Man*. Since metaphor and metonymy inscribe history and defamiliarize it at the same time, the relation between the two gives the reader a clue to the development of subjectivity in the novel.

This difference between metonymy and metaphor can explain why Pecola and Eva invent a double linguistic code in order to differentiate between the female and the male subject. In their story-telling they can transform their positions as victim through a process of splitting the linguistic code and, in this way and to various degrees, they can talk about, abandon, and transform the parts of their lives which hurt. This process is particularly evident in Eva's text which begins in metonymies and ends in metaphors. Her metaphoric code enables her to contrast her isolation to a sense of freedom that she discovers in the stories of other women's lives. This freedom also affects her tenses and enables her to link the past and the future. The bluest eyes Pecola dreams about is a metonymy for the white hegemonic culture that has too often set the standard of beauty and individual worth. When at the beginning of the novel Pecola Breedlove, age nine, arrives at Claudia's home, she already knows that she is unloved by her parents and ignored at school because she is very dark and she does not have the doll-blue eyes of Shirley Temple and Mary Jane. The narrator describes how Pecola has focused her desire for acceptance and love on a different pair of eyes. She believes that a transformation of her eyes into beautiful ones would produce a similar transformation of her parents and the community around her. The narrator depicts the force of a foreign ideal of beauty through a metonymy: blue eyes stand as a *pars pro toto*, a synecdoche for a white little girl whom a racist culture would consider beautiful. Having internalized this ideal, Pecola can only pray for a miracle which, when it occurs, makes her a double outcast since she then becomes excluded from both the black and white communities. The narrator comments on how a "little black girl yearns for the blue eyes of a little white girl, and the horror at the heart of her yearning is exceeded only by the evil of fulfillment" (158). As long as she talks the metonymic language of white America, Pecola remains a victim. Yet, the possibility of self-development had been there if Pecola, like Claudia, had gotten more support from the people around her. Her mother, who could have been a strong force like Claudia's mother, has given up and retired into a world of pre-produced European American images of beauty and order. She lives to care for and clean the house of a white family in a different part of town where she can get some appreciation. To her, Pecola is only an unwanted reminder of her own ugliness and maybe that is why she starts hitting her daughter when Pecola drops the pie in the white family's kitchen and burns herself on the hot filling of the pie. Confronted with her daughter's awkwardness, the mother is abruptly separated from the images she desires and has completely internalized.

Drunk, frustrated, and angry, Cholly Breedlove is no better at nurturing his daughter. Waiting for his violent outbursts, Pecola learns to "Tighten her stomach muscles and ration her breath" (35). The breath motif returns in the rape-scene when release of air is her only response to her father's aggression. "His soul seemed to slip down to his guts and fly out into her, and the gigantic thrust he made into her then provoked the only sound she made—a hollow suck of air in the back of her throat. Like the rapid loss of air from a circus balloon" (128). This sound represents the extent of Pecola's response to what is happening to her. Knowing her community, she sees no arena or avenue within it to deal with her trauma, so she invents a friend with whom she can talk.

In contrast to Eva in Gayl Jones' novel, Pecola never tells her own story in metaphoric language, but the dialogue she spins with her new imaginary friend toward the end of the novel reveals that her father raped her not only once, but twice, and that the second time Pecola did not even try to tell her mother, whom she knew would not have believed her. As the two girlfriends exchange words, Pecola and her double become an extended metaphoric figure of sorts, an allegory of escape. The double that Pecola invents is metaphoric because, since her double dares to do what Pecola has never learned or dared to do—she can protest, she can say no, she can walk away—it combines two unrelated and profoundly different ways of being. The difference between Pecola and her invented friend in turn bridges the concluding image of Pecola as a kind of metaphor. Her metaphoric invention becomes a new kind of trap for her because she is unable to distinguish herself from it. In the end she actually becomes a metaphor to her community and its future. The narrator describes her as a hurt bird that cannot fly but turns toward the blue sky nevertheless and that fills up with that blueness and skyness which it cannot reach. Both model and scapegoat, Pecola also turns into a messianic figure, a savior of sorts, as the community projects its sins and its desire to be clean on her.

Translating herself into a metaphor and becoming a part of the code she seeks to transform, Pecola becomes unable to renew the system she sets up and she consequently cannot become an efficient teacher of a new literacy of self either. Instead, as she gets entangled in her own web, she looses her role as translator and transformer. Because Eva in *Eva's Man* resists identification with her language, her crime, and her madness, she forces the reader to participate in her transformation from mute victim to supreme storyteller and in her shaping a space where she can work as translator of the new literacy of self which she seeks.

In her second novel *Eva's Man* (1976) Gayl Jones tells a story about change and language which has never been properly explored. Shocked by the nature of Eva's crime, most critics strive to come to terms with how she poisoned her lover and bit off his penis.[4] Describing it as a story about a woman's stunted attempts to free herself from sexual and racial oppression, they view it as a story about failure. Richard K. Barksdale, for example, describes it as a "story of the sexual maturation, development, and downfall" of Eva (401) while Jerry W. Ward, Jr. explains how "Eva does not acquire a whole sense of personhood in her formative years. Woman merely responds to the terms presented by the environment in which she is located at any given time" (101). Such judgments reflect a tendency on the part of the critics to see Eva as a biological woman and not as a self-producing text. They also tend to reduce her to a Pygmalion figure, an object mainly shaped by forces outside of her. In contrast, I want to focus on Eva as a searching agent, whose subjectivity remains a utopian text. As a female character repeatedly violated by men, she is silenced and deformed, but as a female subject finding and shaping her genealogy, she is a rich source of women's collective knowledge and oral culture. Building on the narrative richness of that culture, Eva finds words of her own and becomes an artist; her strange story contains the promise of a utopian female subjectivity which she only intuits.

Earlier critics on *Eva's Man* never confront Eva as a story-teller. Their views, acute as they may be in other ways, fail to account for the dramatic change within the language in which Eva tells her story. The striking contrast between the tense, almost naturalistic, realism of the first half of the novel and the haunting, brilliant images of the second part has been left unresolved mainly because most critics have viewed Eva's story-telling as a failure also.[5] I will argue that the key to a better understanding of the novel lies in the difference within Eva's language. As Eva approaches the part of her story when she kills and mutilates Davis, she produces a new and different voice built on images which she inherits from other women and the stories about them. Rediscovering and reevaluating a female oral culture, she finds a richness of images which allows her to write her story and which, ultimately, saves her from destruction.[6] Simultaneously, as she renews this tradition through the splitting of the linguistic code, she wedges this renewal into the system she has used.

A woman who murders and mutilates her lover must be mad, so stripped even of responsibility for her action, Eva is put in a psychiatric prison.[7] Doubly oppressed as a woman and as an insane person, she attempts to understand her situation, first through a linear and chronological (hi)story, then through images that combine the past with the future. Her palimpsestic collection of images produces a space where both the past and the future coexist which ultimately shows the regressive limitations of chronological mode. Eva's search for a female subjectivity is concomitant with the production of a new literacy of self and text necessary for understanding why she abandons that mode. This new literacy blurs the distance between binary distinctions such as sane and insane, and it provokes the uncertainty which surrounds the issue of whether Eva produces an oral or a written text.[8] The first part of her story, which deals with how her family moved from Georgia to New York, is roughly chronological. The move has detrimental consequences for the family, particularly for the women. In the isolated exposure of the big city ghetto, Eva's mother finds stimulation in a lover, and Eva is repeatedly sexually abused by boys and men. When she tries to defend herself through acts of violence, she is put in a penitentiary while her abuser goes free, and so she learns early that society is dominated by men.[9] They write the law and execute justice accordingly. Eva first responds to this violence with silence.

This silence, the lacking female signifier, is the most striking consequence of the reification of women in the society Eva describes. Throughout the novel, Eva often refuses to answer questions and she rarely volunteers any information. Aggressively non-communicative, she remains silent even during the trial where she stands accused of violence against the man, Moses Tripp, who assaulted her. In his analysis of *Eva's Man* in *Fingering the Jagged Grain*, Byerman points out that this "silence is her refusal to rationalize her behavior in terms of the system she has so pointedly assaulted" (184). The female silence shows an Eva who refuses to participate in Moses' law. It also stands in direct opposition to the narrating subject's pursuit of voice, her struggle, not only with demeaning physical and sexual experiences, but also with demanding problems of how to produce her sense of subjectivity in language. It is paradoxical that men, who intended to punish her, provide her with a space where she is sheltered from masculinist aggression, and where she can begin a search for words of her own. Her archeological exploration reveals not a personal experience and an individual expression, but a communal female experience shared over generations and a collection of women's stories which help her produce her own.

Eva's chronological tale of male abuse is interspersed with stories about other women and their lives, such as Medina, the puzzling woman called the queen bee, Eva's great-grandmother, grandmother, and mother, Miss Billie and her daughter, Charlotte. These women form a link over generations, and they provide Eva with a female oral culture which allows them, emotionally and physically, to share tenderness and knowledge. The oral tradition allows women from different generations to form a community without boundaries of time or space. But this culture is seriously threatened. Since the two young women portrayed in the novel, Eva and Charlotte, lack children to whom they can pass on this source of knowledge, the oral female culture can survive only in written form. This insight partly informs the urgency of Eva's attempts to find her own words: if only in the second-hand fashion characteristic of texts, her book is the new body and the new repository of women's culture.

Illustrating these women's sense of history and of interconnectedness Eva establishes a metaphoric chain of memories that weaves the past with the future. In one memory, the Gypsy Medina comes to Eva's Great-Grandmama's house begging for food, and in another, which I will discuss later, Eva links the memories of her crime to the crime of the biblical Eve who also ate a forbidden fruit. The intertextual allusions to the biblical Eve exemplify a female literary history, while the memories of Medina spin a tale about the women in Eva's immediate family. These stories reflect the two sides of Eva, who is both the supreme teller of her tale and the subjected victim within it. In the first memory Eva relates how her Great-Grandmother told her husband about meeting Medina. She says to him that Medina had time in the palm of her hand. Unable to understand the implications of this female time, he teases her and asks his wife if the Gypsy wanted money put in her hand. This embarrasses the Great-Grandmother who denies the issue of payment and says that the Gypsy wanted her to kiss the palm of her hand. With this kiss, Medina and Eva's Great-Grandmother share a common metaphor for female power and the bond between women. Women carry time in their palms, an image which suggests that for them, biology is not necessarily destiny but a choice for plurality, a possibility of fusing difference and similarity. This possibility is further emphasized since the two women belong to different cultures. Eva's mother's friend from North Carolina, Miss Billie, echoes the same image when she tells Eva that she has both history and future in her hand. Being named after the Gypsy, Eva Medina who tells the story carries on the fusing tendencies in women's culture.

But Charlotte and Eva belong to the last generation of women who share the oral female culture. Eva's mother's friend Billie, for example, tells Eva about her ancestors. Miss Billie wears five wooden bracelets on her arm and when Eva starts school, she gives her one of them and tells her that she must stay true to her ancestors, that she must stay true to both past and future generations. Miss Billie's symbolic gift suggests the possibility of an alternative education, and it represents an inheritance of strength and women's culture that in a different kind of environment might have protected Eva. But Eva soon loses the bracelet. Instead, she hangs on to the knife that she gets from Freddie Smoot, a neighbor boy who molests her with a dirty popsicle stick when she is five years old. Later, Eva uses that knife to try to protect herself from Alfonso and from Moses Tripp.

Medina, queen bee and the other women are all stories in Eva's text and may be different projections of her own self. Yet, the genealogy of the metaphors is female. Another of Eva's recurring images is of a woman buried in sand: "She was under sand. And he came and put a hole—not for air—but so he could stick his thing in" (140). Earlier in the novel, Eva remembers that her mother used to talk about how they buried her mother, Eva's grandmother, in the sand and forgot her there. When they finally remembered to dig her out her hearing and eye-sight were permanently damaged. Since the burial-in-the-sand image refers not so much to a specific event, which may or may not have occurred, as to a story about the said event, the genealogy of Eva's images reinforces the unreferential nature of both her metaphors and of history. Eva, the granddaughter, understands that history, both personal and racial, can only be known through narration. Since, most probably, the grandmother-mother-daughter link of orally transferred knowledge will be broken, Eva must now write her story.

The more Eva remembers about the women in her life, past and present, the easier it gets for her to find images for her own experiences. The stories by and about these women provide the possibility of writing the female subject in a different voice. This new voice is heard most clearly in the haunting images of the second part of the novel, such as the one of Mr. Logan. Eva overhears Miss Billie tell her mother about the time when Mr. Logan masturbated in front of Miss Billie when she was a child (12). An old man when Eva grows up, Mr. Logan sits on the landing outside the Canada's apartment registering what takes place in the building. Miss Billie asks Eva if he ever messed with her and she says no, thinking of the boy who did. In Part Two, Eva begins talking about Mr. Logan as an old owl perched on the stairs. The owl, a solitary, nocturnal bird of prey that likes to inhabit empty old buildings is analogous to men such as Alfonso, Moses, and Davis who attach themselves to women who lack a sense of self and who are, in that sense, empty. But the owl-metaphor becomes increasingly hostile as the owl attacks the girl, pins her to the floor, pecks at her and even sucks her blood.[10] The owl-image is symptomatic, and it illustrates a gender division within Eva's metaphoric code. In her system, men are described as birds of prey: hunters, killers, and meat-eaters.[11] In contrast, she usually describes women's actions in terms of fruit. This division recurs in her description of how she kills and mutilates Davis.

Creating a division within the metaphoric code, Eva becomes free to articulate her own sensations and memories, particularly those connected to the murder and mutilation of Davis. Writing about an article somebody wrote in a police magazine, Eva begins her story with a missing version of her crime. Eva herself has never seen this article, but one of the other prisoners tells her that it had two photographs, one of the dead man and another of Eva. Suppressing the text of the article, Eva gives the reader a clue to the central issue of her story, which is, I believe, to explore the gap between living and writing, between an event and the story about it. Moreover, the suppressed article is of interest because it appropriates both Eva's act of murder, and, since it includes her photo, her body. Eva also distinguishes between the two. She dislikes the photo of Davis, but not the photo of herself. So from the beginning of her story, Eva establishes her own hierarchy in which her acts are more important than her body. She never could protect her physical body, but she wants to guard the imprints she made on Davis' body and the body of text that she produces. She needs to protect her "texts" on Davis' body and on the page. Writing on a male body and on a page, Eva reverses the traditional imagery of men writing (on) the female body as if it were a blank page.[12] The freedom with which she reverses these roles reminds the reader of her surname, Canada, a name which, as Dixon points out, refers to "the promised land for fugitive slaves" (245). It also suggests that, in writing histories as well as stories, women are still searching for the promised land, and that for them, possibly, the shape of both the promise and the land is different.

The missing official newspaper version of what Eva did is symptomatic of both her illness and her skill as a story-teller. It also suggests a diegetic cure. When Eva begins to formulate her experiences of

the murder and molestation of her lover, she reaches deep into a female
and textual history, and she compares her crime with that of Eve in the
Garden of Eden. She uses imagery which evokes the biblical story of Eve
who eats the forbidden apple. Initially, she also upholds the distinction
between fruit as female and the male organ as alien to her. But as she
finds words to describe her experiences, Eva transfers the male body from
one code to another, from sausage to apple and plum.[13] Susan Rubin
Suleiman discusses how an "integral part of the new 'feminine' poetics is
to reappropriate, by means of ironic rereadings—and rewritings—the
dominant cultural productions of the past" (18). But Eva's intertextual
allusion to the biblical Eve is not ironic. Her repetition of Eve's act—
eating the forbidden fruit—presents a powerful rewriting of the biblical
story. Eva searches for ways to rewrite the myth and to make it
worthwhile to kneel down in prayer. This time she desires a solitary Eden
where she can eat the fruit (and the snake?), invent a new language, and
clear a space for a different knowledge. In the new paradise Eva will have
power, a power that Medina has bequeathed to her when she said that God
is God "because he can turn milk and sweat into blood" (138).

Victimized and molded by male imagination, the women in Eva's
world often lack power. According to Medina, women can usurp male
power and create a new Eden through a combination of violence and
creativity. The murder of Davis and Eva's search for words of her own to
describe it are such acts of usurpation. Violated and violent, Eva eats the
forbidden fruit. Transgressing both sexual and textual limits, she
simultaneously destroys and creates. In the interview with Claudia Tate,
Gayl Jones dwells on such double, oxymoronic experiences when she
explains how negative feelings can give birth to positive ones.

> What comes out in my work, in those particular novels [*Corregidora* and
> *Eva's Man*], is an emphasis on brutality. Something else is also suggested
> in them that will perhaps be pursued in other works, namely the alternative
> to brutality, which is tenderness. Although the main focus of *Corregidora*
> and *Eva's Man* is on the blues relationships or relationships involving
> brutality, there seems to be a growing understanding—working itself out

especially in *Corregidora*—of what is required in order to be genuinely
tender. Perhaps brutality enables one to recognize what tenderness is. (98)

Gayl Jones emphasizes how brutality and tenderness are connected in
Corregidora, but she has also showed their interdependence in *Eva's Man*.
It can be traced particularly through Eva's increasing reliance on
metaphoric images and her growing relationship to her cellmate Elvira
Moody.

Eva's response to Elvira's sexual invitations develops from
unwillingness to acceptance. In the beginning, Eva rejects all of Elvira's
advances, but Elvira does not give up easily. Later, Eva reacts when
Elvira pulls off a scab on her knee, and Elvira is quick to notice that Eva
has started to care. Elvira is the first woman to give Eva an answer to a
question that has troubled her ever since she was a child when her mother
told her that women open their legs and they will never again be satisfied
until they do it again. Elvira is independent from men and wonders about a
woman's ability to close her legs again, which is a gesture of power and a
control of her own body which Eva has never even thought about.

Elvira represents an alternative to the power of the phallus, but Eva is
not ready to embrace this freedom yet. First she must discover that her
body and the body of language are tools that actually can belong to her.
The proximity of her textual and sexual discoveries suggests their
interdependence and echoes Hélène Cixous' fluent argument for feminine
writing.[14]

A feminine text cannot not be more than subversive: if it writes itself it
is in volcanic heaving of the old "real" property crust. In ceaseless
displacement. She must write herself because, when the time comes for her
liberation, it is the invention of a *new, insurgent* writing that will allow her
to put the breaks and indispensable changes into effect in her history. At
first, individually, on two separable levels:—woman, writing herself, will
go back to this body that has been worse than confiscated, a body replaced
with a disturbing stranger, sick or dead, who so often is a bad influence, the

cause and place of inhibitions. By censuring the body, breath and speech
are censored at the same time.

    To write—the act that will "realise" the un-censored relationship of
woman to her sexuality . . . ("Sorties," 116).

At the end of the novel Eva has discovered this intimate relationship
between her body and her voice. She is ready to both break her silence
and to welcome Elvira into her bed: "'Tell me when it feels sweet, Eva.
Tell me when it feels sweet, honey.' I leaned back, squeezing her face
between my legs, and told her, 'Now.'" (177). Even though the reader
cannot know whether Eva's response to Elvira repeats her earlier
submissive behavior toward men, the word "now" suggests a more positive
possibility that Eva re-enters a female realm where past and present coexist. Together with other women and with the help of their stories, Eva
has found both sexual and textual freedom.

    Eva's process of liberation must be viewed in the context of her
pursuit of a language which intimates a different and female subjectivity
which is, as yet, mostly unknown. Even so, some critics cannot resist the
temptation to interpret Eva's metaphors. For example, Ward argues that
Eva "symbolizes womanhood in blood and bread, in private correlatives
(man/owl; orgasm/river; power/the Medusa) and establishes resemblances
between food and defecation" (102). But Eva's metaphors—though clearly
symbolic in nature—are not necessarily private or referential. The reader
cannot easily translate them into a specific meaning without reducing their
suggestive and secretive nature. Indicating the lack of referential certainty
and identification, Eva's images stand as ciphers suggesting that notions of
"certainty" and "identity" like "chronology" cannot free her. These
images show the power of the narrating female subject to present herself
and her possible future self as both a mysterious and, as yet, a mostly
unwritten text.

    Through these images, Eva also challenges the dominant myth that
women are connected to literal language while men master the figurative;
women are linked to nature while men transcend the natural world and
reach metaphysical truth. Margaret Homans argues, for example, that

> the differential valuations of literal and figurative originate in the way our
> culture constructs masculinity and femininity, for if the literal is associated
> with the feminine, the more highly valued figurative is associated with the
> masculine. To take something literally is to get it wrong, while to have a
> figurative understanding of something is the correct intellectual stance (5).

In order to formulate her unspeakable experience, Eva reaches for a figurative language, an act which reverses the dominant myth of gendered language. In their poetic richness, the images also present the narrative subject's desire to create an alternative world to her poverty-ridden and repressive past.[15]

On the one hand, the female subject has both the power and the desire to suppress a master key that could explain her secretive metaphors. On the other hand, she links the images to a past history of women. Eva's pursuit to fill in the blank space of the female subject, to draw the map of her uncharted geography, takes the shape of a detective story. The story and the subject split in two as Eva the subject-narrator is trying to understand the whats and the whys of Eva the subject-protagonist. As she clarifies the epistemological uncertainties surrounding Eva's actions, however, the narrating subject raises a more disturbing ontological doubt linked to the question of why Eva killed Davis. She says that she killed him because of his way of being. His mode of existence threatened hers to such a degree that she had to erase him; yet he fills the pages of her book. This double bind illustrates the complex position of all oppressed story-tellers who in order to condemn such crimes as slavery, and racial and sexual violations must reproduce them on the page. It also contributes to the sense of claustrophobia in the novel and shows how difficult Eva's situation is. In removing Davis' "being," Eva attempts to replace one ontology with another, and she creates an uncertainty which adds to the postmodernist quality of *Eva's Man*. Brian McHale's lucid study *Postmodernist Fiction* proposes that "the dominant of postmodernist fiction is *ontological*" (10).[16] For Eva, however, the shifting ontological systems are gendered: her search for a different mode of being is a search for a female subjectivity which writes itself, not simply as other in reaction to a male mode of being, but in a utopian marginal realm which is as yet merely intuitional. Eva's shifting ontologies can be traced in her moving away from a metonymic language which she associates with male being toward a metaphoric language for which she provides only a history and a genealogy, but not a master key.[17]

The sliding movement from one category to another, from metonymy to metaphor, becomes a link in Eva's development both as a subject and as a writer. She uses one major metonymy to indicate her position as Other in the first half of the book: her own empty eyes. In more traditional Western literature, a character's eyes commonly express somebody's essential being while, at the same time, they mirror the world. Like a transparent window, they allow a smooth and constructive exchange. In *Eva's Man*, this window works only one way so that Eva can see out, but nobody can see in. Supplying no entry into the subject, the eyes function both as a boundary and as a sign for the yet unwritten and unformed female subject. Lacking any knowledge of the subject's ontological status, only the gaze of the other temporarily defines her: girl, woman, whore, monster. Onto her opaque eyes everybody projects their wishes and fears. Most of the men read their sexual desire for Eva in her eyes, but during their stay together Davis comes to fear a certain look on Eva's face which he cannot deny or interpret. Temporarily, Eva can resist the interpretive gaze of the other, but her opaque look signals no substantial alternative; it functions as a sign for a lacking female culture and subjectivity. Her look kills him in a symbolic way, an act which probably would have sufficed had she been permitted a sense of self within but, in order to create herself and a new symbolic order, Eva has to destroy the old one. Like her writing, her revolt is both literal and figurative, both retrospective and utopian. Remembering that the Gypsy Medina had a similar experience, she also ties the notion of the telling eyes to sexual power and to the female community that knows how to use that something in the eyes that looks at men and makes them think that they are wanted.

Eva's story is no more a simple success-story than it is simply a story of a woman's failure to adjust and prosper in a male-dominated society.

Eva is both a "subjectifier" and a "subjectified," and the reader's knowledge about her takes shape in the relational space between the two. In *Eva's Man* the double subject's process of liberation has a chiasmic shape: while the subjectifier searches for a new language—which also is her mother tongue—the subjectified is almost destroyed by an alien, male tongue. This double movement dissolves into the plethora of opaque but suggestive images at the end of the novel. These images reflect a moving away from referentiality and interpretation, suggesting the disappearance of "meaning." Having offered the reader the illusion of order—a life-story in other words—the double subject withdraws her promise and dissolves into a series of metaphors which threaten the position of both subject and reader. *Eva's Man* turns dangerously poetic, or "seductive," to use Jean Baudrillard's term.[18] It explodes in a colorful web of inscrutable images which indicate the foreign qualities of the female subject. The process of writing her story in her own words has taken Eva away from a hierarchic and binary language where she was almost hidden and silenced. No longer pretending that she can produce an interpretable text, she negates the processes of both repression and liberation. She fills the vacuum with a plurality of images, many of which are scary. But the frightening quality of these images cannot compare to the terror radiating around the subjectless Eva with opaque eyes seen at the beginning of the novel. Her newly-found images may bewilder and frighten the reader, but they promise the production of a new female community and culture, of new female tenderness and knowledge.

A Separate Genre

In chapter two, I illustrated how *Invisible Man* reverses many fundamental steps of the classical *Bildungsroman*, but the double oppression facing the black female subject makes the female African American narrative of *Bildung* invert or subvert the classical model in more far-reaching ways. The female subject, the voices of the narrators, the narrative structure, the passivity of the protagonist, the marking of the passage from girl to woman, the movement inwards rather than outwards, the development from a silent subject position to one of mad discourse, and the eventual fragmentation of the traditional essential self—the African American female narrative of *Bildung* constructs all of these key moments in different ways. Barbara Johnson argues that the "law of genre . . . is also, of course, a law of gender" (1987: 33). And, we might want to add, of culture. Formulating the experiences of black women, the African American female narrative of *Bildung* forms a separate genre which reflects the pursuit of a language that can capture the experiences of a community which has been systematically excluded from or parasitically exploited by the white Western paradigm[19] and, in the words of Geta LeSeur, "the sense of 'two-ness,' of belonging to a minority group, and being female" (29). The genealogy of this genre remains to be traced. By focusing on two texts which capture extreme violations and reactions, I attempt merely to show the need for a paradigm different from the European American one.

As a genre the classical *Bildungsroman* was shaped to shut out the experience of all female subjects (most of which return through the backdoors of fear and desire). Even though there was no lack of novels dealing with the maturation of female protagonists at the time the classical genre was named, traditionally the classical *Bildungsroman* is always defined in terms of its male protagonists. The term *Bildungsroman* was first used before 1820 in Germany by a professor in classical philosophy, Karl Morgenstern (Martini 44). At that time Jane Austen had published all of her major novels, including *Emma* (1816), which can be called a female *Bildungsroman*. Even so most scholars and critics of the classical *Bildungsroman* choose Goethe's *Wilhelm Meister* as the *Ur*-type of the genre and they tend to focus on the passage from boyhood to manhood. In *Seasons of Youth*, Jerome Hamilton Buckley argues, for example, that "the gentlemanly ideal" is basic to the genre (20). Randolph P. Shaffner's study, which covers only male protagonists, reflects the same tendency. The Swedish scholar Tommy Olofsson studies three *Bildungsromane* including *A Portrait of the Artist as a Young Man*, and agrees with Georg Lukács that the classical *Bildungsroman* is "the form of *manly maturation*"

(28).[20] In *The Bluest Eye* and *Eva's Man*, however, not only the respective protagonists, Pecola and Eva, are female, but so are the narrators and almost all the other major figures in the novels. Male characters are only presented as either active violators of women or as passive and helpless figures in the background.

The African American female narrative of *Bildung* differs from the classical model not only through the use of female protagonists as central characters but also through the striking use of narrative voices which rarely can be narrowed to a single subject. Turning the narrative into a communal, unhierarchical space for many voices, the fragmentation of the narrative voice changes the patterns of power and domination within the African American female narrative of *Bildung*. Karla F. Holloway has focused on this aspect in her argument that "Black women writers seem to concentrate on shared ways of saying" (7). The structure of *Eva's Man* allows a chorus of voices and stories to add to the hysterical tone and tempo of the novel. In a similar way, the series of unidentified narrators which succeed Claudia as narrator reflect and illustrate Pecola's increasingly destructive passage into namelessness and fragmentation. It might be tempting to argue that the novel is focused on the narrator Claudia's process of maturation rather than on Pecola's, that the novel describes the *Bildung* of Claudia rather than the (anti)*Bildung* of Pecola, but such an argument does not solve the problem of Pecola's central role in the novel and the formulation of the title, which seems to refer to Pecola. Even though Claudia opens the novel by describing her own maturation process as one of "adjustment not improvement" (22), neither the focus nor the narrative voice stays with Claudia. The chorus of blending female voices and narrators suggests that the experiences and the struggles of African American women bridge over generations and separates the African American female narrative of *Bildung* from the classical genre.

These narrative voices also invert the traditionally autobiographical mode of the classical *Bildungsroman* which is generally considered an autobiographical genre. Buckley argues, for example, that "the typical novel of youth is strongly autobiographical and therefore subject at any time to intrusions from areas of the author's experiences beyond the dramatic limits of fiction" (23-24). In a series of distinctions between the classical *Bildungsroman* and other closely related types of novels, Shaffner likewise links what he calls "the apprentice novel" with other biographical and autobiographical types of novels. He concludes with Dilthey that the aim of the *Bildungsroman* is to elevate the life of the protagonist to a universal level while the biographical novels remain personal. He writes that in "the apprenticeship novel we witness the apprentice transcend his particular individuality to achieve universality" (13). His need to make this distinction reveals how closely linked the two forms are to him. *The Bluest Eye* and *Eva's Man* are narratives of *Bildung* and, at least partly, first person narratives, but they are not in any overt way autobiographical; the shifting narrative focus reinforces the impersonal texture of these novels and the particularity of the genre.

The status and involvement of the subject shows another main difference between the two genres. Shaffner writes that the protagonist's active involvement distinguishes the *Bildungsroman* from psychological novels in general when he says that the "central character of the novel of development, or psychological novel, evolves unconsciously, whereas the protagonist of the apprenticeship novel matures in full awareness of his formation" (11). Likewise, Susan Howe argues that the *Bildungsroman* deals with "a more or less conscious attempt on the part of the hero to integrate his powers, to cultivate himself by his experience" (6). Also, Oloffson maintains that in "the *Bildungsroman* the external events, the happenings of the world, are in consequence subordinated to the inner development of the hero" (25). In stark contrast, the protagonists in *The Bluest Eye* and *Eva's Man* do not actively participate in their own developments. Pecola withdraws from any active involvement, and Eva remains aggressively passive and silent. *The Bluest Eye* begins with a description of the physical realities and the atmosphere in Claudia's home, which it later contrasts to those of Pecola's. Claudia's family may be lacking in a material sense, but they are rich in social reinforcement, culture, and love. They talk to each other, they have names and established relationships, and on very bad days they know how to sing the blues.

But this sympathetic picture of that family is somewhat marred by the difference they make between the two strangers who arrive in their house. Mr. Henry, who rents a room in the house, gets both attention and space and sympathy. Until it becomes clear that Mr. Henry is fond of the girls in a perverted way, he is allowed to joke and play around with the children. In contrast, Pecola arrives at Claudia's home without a name or any luggage. The narrator contrasts the friendly scene with Mr. Henry to a brief statement that "she" slept in the sisters' bed. Her name is added a few sentences later, followed in turn by her position in the household as "a case," a non-paying charge whom the MacTeers take in out of sympathy and out of pride in the community spirit. While Mr. Henry gets a room, Pecola, who is placed between Claudia and Frieda in the girls' bed, does not even get a symbolic space of her own. Pecola's poverty and dependency is further emphasized because she does not even bring a change of clothes or a nightgown. In both a material and a psychological sense, Pecola is uninvolved in the shaping of her position. As different narrative voices take turns to tell her story, they reflect her lack of a place from which to speak. Likewise, Eva, in *Eva's Man*, grows up with her own parents in a small apartment where she has little or no space of her own. She sleeps on the sofa in the living room at night where she overhears her parents have sex, and she must move around the apartment at other people's will. The lack of a physical space of their own indicates their marginal position in their own maturation stories and it suggests the narrowness of the two characters' future prospects as well.

The classical *Bildungsroman* is constructed around the controversial desire of the protagonist, such as Wilhelm Meister's desire for the world of the theater. This desire fuels the hero with activity and aggression and prompts him to venture out into the world seeking his own path in life. The strength of his initial desire often equals his ultimate amount of social and personal power. In Jones' and Morrison's novels, the African American female subject differs dramatically from this picture in that her desires are unformed and unexpressed, and the strength of her suppressed desires seems to equal her ultimate social and personal victimization. Pecola, for example, is passive at home and in school, and she suffers silently. Her only existential act is an act of self-obliteration: drinking three quarts of milk a day, she can forget herself in front of the picture of Shirley Temple on the milkmug. Her passive response to Claudia and Frieda, her peers and equals, even more strongly suggests her inability to actively shape her own situation. In these novels, the female African American subject inverts the self-assertiveness of the protagonist in the classical *Bildungsroman*.

The male hero of the classical *Bildungsroman* often marks his physical passage into manhood with an active conquest, a sexual experience, when he makes love for the first time often with a woman who is linked to his desired future. So Wilhelm Meister makes love to Mariane, dreaming of a future they will have together building the national theater of Germany. Pecola marks her physical passage from girlhood to womanhood with her first menstruation. This passage from childhood to womanhood is clearly announced, but it is something that happens *to* the female subject, not something that she actively pursues through an act of desire. Pecola's passage, then, emphasizes the relative passivity of the female subject. In the end it is Claudia, not Pecola, who carries in "the little-girl-gone-to-woman pants" (28). The silence of these little girls also indicates that the community around them is not strong enough to teach them the stories of the past or to listen to their stories of violence. They never learn the shared ways of speaking, and they don't seem have anybody to confide in or to ask all the questions about sexuality and womanhood that trouble them. Eva has to wait until she is in prison before she gets a reasonable answer to a question she has carried around since girlhood. Pecola is equally puzzled when the MacTeer sisters tell her that her menstruation means that she can have children if somebody loves her. Since she lacks any experience of love, she has no strategy how to deal with the conditional and nobody to ask. Her passive formulation (how to make somebody love you) shows that the physical rite of spring only strengthens Pecola's vulnerability. Without an understanding of human feelings and sexuality, she becomes an easy target for sexual exploitation.

The victimization of the female subject is also reflected in the ambiguous relationship she has to other characters. The passivity of

Pecola and Eva allows other characters to gain in importance and stature in the novels. Whereas in the classical *Bildungsroman* the external and internal growth of the protagonist dominates the focus, the African American female subject in these texts shares the limelight with other characters who become equally, if not more, noticeable in the eyes of the reader. In *The Bluest Eye*, the maturation story of Pecola is intertwined with the maturation stories of Claudia, Frieda, Maureen Peal, and Pecola's parents, to mention a few. In contrast to the classical male hero, Pecola retires deeper within herself as she is shuffled from one place to another, thus exemplifying one of the most commonly identified traits of the female *Bildungsroman*.[21] Abel, Hirsch, and Langland argue, for example, that the novels of female development "typically substitute inner concentration for active accommodation, rebellion, or withdrawal" (8). The inner lives of Pecola and Eva cannot, however, be described as concentrated or enriching. Even though Eva's story is crowded with other people's views, it seems only to strengthen the impression of inner emptiness and division. The female subject is represented as an empty space where the cultural fragments have no perceivable design or purpose. For Eva the many stories turn into a whirlwind that she seems unable to control or use in any constructive way, whereas Pecola's inner life is described as a series of desires to become an other, to become white, to become blue-eyed, to project and reflect the ideals of an alien and oppressive culture.

"Confinement to inner life, no matter how enriching, threatens a loss of public activity," write Abel, Hirsch, and Langland (8). This is one of the strongest differences between the female African American narrative of *Bildung* as it is projected in these novels and the classical *Bildungsroman*. In the classical genre the young man can define himself through a series of defiant actions which in turn puts pressure on the society to change so that when he is ready to return to society he can do so without feeling compromised. This possibility of having it both ways, of both being part of and differ from the surrounding society is reflected in the criticism. Focusing on the development of the individual in his own right, Buckley argues that the hero "has at least discovered the importance of self-assertion, indeed self-creation, through defiant action and courageous gesture" (16-17). Shaffner, too, discusses the importance of being and becoming but places a stronger emphasis on goal-orientation, on "the idea of becoming, both in a definite sense and with a definite goal in mind" (8). The goal, as he sees it, is one of social adjustment and professional assertion. The hero must find a useful role in society. Still, even for Shaffner the development of the individual is more important than that of society. Clarifying his preference, he suggests that "Self-formation against a background of all the influences that the world can offer, therefore, identifies the apprenticeship novel" (11). Similarly, Olofsson posits that a "genuine process of *Bildung* consists not only of assimilation but also of active self-creation" (21).

Female subjects like Pecola and Eva are effectively excluded from any useful interaction with a patriarchal and racist society; therefore, they are also denied the possibility of bringing something productive to their societies. In the European paradigm, *Bildung* is not a goal in its own right; to be considered successful, it must produce productive social beings. Since women are generally considered productive only in a reproductive sense this too reflects the gender-bias in the classical version. Olofsson emphasizes the pragmatic impulse in the classical paradigm, when he writes that "the harmonious development of the individual's unique traits should not only or even primarily serve to make people happy each in his or her own right; *Bildung* should lead to a productive life in a social community with other unique and free beings. The underlying ideology is that of liberalism" (20).

This pattern of external experience and internal growth originates in Wilhelm von Humboldt's distinction between *Anbildung* and *Ausbildung* (Stahl 44). This distinction is hard to maintain in English since the English language does not permit it, but for the purposes of clarification I propose the translations "enveloping" and "developing." *Anbildung*, enveloping, comes from without. The term signifies knowledge brought from without, what is taught in schools, what belongs to the public sphere of knowledge. Therefore, the term *Anbildung* is inappropriate in designating the realm of female knowledge and love discussed later in this chapter, since that realm has never been included in the public, male-dominated sphere.

Ausbildung, on the other hand, belongs to the private sphere; it depicts what comes from within the individual. It stands for the development of the unique capacities of a particular individual. This term, too, is inappropriate in talking about the female subject whose unique properties are un(der)developed and unformulated. The African American female narrative of *Bildung* with its strong emphasis on a female community and culture passed on through generations disrupts this distinction between self and world, and suggests a different pattern of interaction between the individual and her world.

Full of bitterness, violence, and silence, both *The Bluest Eye* and *Eva's Man* challenge the world and these communities. Depicted as virtually ego-less examples of "transparent" or nonexistent texts of self, their violated female characters are abandoned by their communities. The novels show that identities—cultural, gendered, racial, historical, national, social, (in)sane—are learned and must be taught. Their power lies in the capturing of the void inside and the tracing of what is put in its place. Ultimately creating an alternative community in her mind, Pecola fills that void with an imaginary reality and makes her new friend produce the nourishing and ego-strengthening quarrels she needs to draw the limits and to give her a familial place of resistance. Had this strategy been a temporary one, it might have led Pecola back into her community, but the irreversibility of the damage is signaled through her becoming the metaphor that fills the void, the bird that cannot fly. Patrick Bryce Bjork comments on how Pecola, "like Ovid's Philomela, has had her tongue cut out by an act which has inverted the natural order of her life . . . . thus like Philomela who turns into a nightingale, Pecola, too, tries to transform herself and transcend the mutilation of her life" (53). To fill the void of her increasing absence, the narrator describes a community that sucks strength and vigor from it. Thus the function of Pecola's void is to bring out the void in the community. In contrast, Eva's void gets filled up with a psychotic vertigo of fragmented women's stories and, however ambiguous the closing scene is, she is still at its center, literally embracing the single representative of the female community available to her and changing her perspective from the past to the present tense. Both these novels describe the fragile limits of the traditionally supportive women's culture and show that, to protect their young and to teach them shared ways of saying, women must learn to listen for and to incorporate the often painful stories of difference within their community.

NOTES

1   In the essay "Coming to Writing," p. 7.
2   See chapter one, note 13.
3   I am grateful to Professor Carrie Jaures Noland who suggested that metonymy reflects and defamiliarizes history in a paper on the French poet René Char at the Twentieth Century Literature Conference in Louisville, KY, 1991.
4   Most critics call her act an act of castration which, properly speaking, it is not. The lack of a term to describe her crime adds resonance to the main point of my argument that in order to form a sense of subjectivity, Eva must invent a new language.
5   Melvin Dixon, for example, believes that "Eva never gains control over her voice, her past, or her identity" (245). Ward points out that for Eva "Language is not sufficient. It has to be extended as visual thought—woman is queen bee, for example, because visual thinking allows Eva to grasp meaning more completely" (100) and that "the very fictionality of her [Gayl Jones'] fiction reimmerses us in man's struggle with the greatest demon in his mind: language" (102).   Keith E. Byerman mentions that "Eva is describing, in increasingly incomprehensible terms, her poisoning and castrating of the man with whom she lived" (447). None of these critics sheds much light over the differences and difficulties with Eva's use of language.
6   In her excellent critical study *Liberating Voices: Oral Tradition in African American Literature* (Cambridge, Mass.: Harvard UP 1991), Gayl Jones suggests that in *The Autobiography of Miss Jane Pittman* Ernest Gaines "realizes the potential of voice that was only suggested by Zora Neal Hurston in *Their Eyes Were Watching God*" (161).   But I think that Jones herself has developed a significant response to the problem of a female and an African American voice in the creation of the first-person narrator in *Eva's Man*.   In *Moorings and Metaphors: Figures of Culture and Gender in Black*

Women's Literature (New Brunswick, NJ: Rutgers UP 1992) Karla
F. C. Holloway argues that voice, "shared ways of saying" (7), is
one of the strongest features of black women's writing. Holloway
discusses *Corregidora*, but many of her conclusions are highly
relevant to *Eva's Man*.

7   On the female subject and madness, see Shoshana Felman's
"Women and Madness: The Critical Phallacy," *The Feminist
Reader: Essays in Gender and the Politics of Literary Criticism*, ed.
Catherine Belsey and Jane Moore (London: Macmillan, 1989) 133-
153.

8   It is my sense that Eva is a writer, a grammatologist, who places
writing over speech. Eva's attempts to become "literate" illustrate a
contemporary version of the long-standing African American
struggle toward literacy. See for example Valerie Smith's
indispensable study *Self-Discovery and Authority in Afro-American
Narrative* (Cambridge, Mass.: Harvard UP, 1987).

9   Byerman emphasizes the gender difference regarding what is
considered criminal and/or acceptable behavior. He maintains that
Eva's experiences and the stories of the queen bee only reinforce
"the view that women are by nature sinful, that they are responsible
for the evil in the world. Original sin, in some cosmic way, has
attached itself to the female gender. Eva is thus further encouraged
to believe that a woman can never be innocent, even if she has done
nothing" (454). This view reflects that of Eva's psychiatrist whose
analysis of Eva's behavior is simplistic: "You thought you were a
bad woman, so you went out and got you a bad man" (174). Eva
responds to this idea by getting violent. Her reaction could be a sign
of two things: either his interpretation is correct, and she resents the
mirror image or, more believable, her version of "the truth" is so far
removed from his that she resents his attempts at "writing her
script." Other African American authors explore the same theme.
In an interview with John O'Brien, Alice Walker explains that in
writing *The Third Life of Grange Copeland* she wanted "to explore

the relationship between men and women, and why women are always condemned for doing what men do as an expression of their masculinity. Why are women so easily 'tramps' and 'traitors' when men are heroes for engaging in the same activity?" *Interviews with Black Writers* (New York: Liveright, 1973) 197.

10   The image of the owl occurs three times. "The owl corners me, lays me on the floor, begins to dig and peck" (138). "The owl is perched on the stairs. 'I've come to protect this woman,' he says. But he turns into a cock, and descends. A lemon between his legs. She has made the juice run" (144). "An owl sucks my blood. I am bleeding underneath my nails. An old owl sucks my blood. He gives me fruit in my palms. We enter the river again . . . together" (176).

11   It is interesting to note that the man Eva marries is named James Hunn, but his nickname is Hawk. Eva comments on how "after we married I always called him James" (105).

12   Susan Gubar, "'The Blank Page' and the Issues of Female Creativity," *Writing and Sexual Difference*, ed. Elizabeth Abel (Chicago: The U of Chicago P, 1982) 73-93. She argues that this "model of the pen-penis writing on the virgin page participates in a long tradition identifying the author as a male who is primary and the female as his passive creation—a secondary object lacking autonomy, endowed with often contradictory meaning but denied intentionality" (77). Gubar also discusses how "one of the primary and most resonant metaphors provided by the female body is blood, and cultural forms of creativity are often experienced as a painful wounding" (78). Eva's preoccupation with blood and bleeding as well as her description of her mutilation of Davis' body fit within this pattern; her transgression is cultural and textual, and it takes the shape of a terrible wounding. See also Elizabeth A. Meese, "Defiance: The Body (of) Writing/The Writing (of) Body," *Crossing the Double-Cross: The Practice of Feminist Criticism* (Chapel Hill: The U of North Carolina P, 1986) 115-132. Barbara Johnson also makes a significant point when she argues that "The very equation of

the woman's body with the blank page implies that the woman's body is white (indeed, of a whiteness no actual bodies possess)." (267) "Is Female to Male as Ground Is to Figure?" *Feminism and Psychoanalysis* ed. Richard Feldstein and Judith Roof. (Ithaca: Cornell UP, 1989) 255-268.

13 For a discussion about male and female consumption, cannibalism, and disorderly eating in *Eva's Man*, see my article "The Forbidden Apple and Female Disorderly Eating: Three Versions of Eve," *The Disorderly Eaters: Texts in Self-Empowerment* (University Park: The Pennsylvania State UP, 1992) ed. Lilian R. Furst and Peter W. Graham.

14 After reading Kadiatu Kanneh's charge of a racist colonial metaphorics in Irigaray's and Cixous' writings in "Love, Mourning, and Metaphor: Terms of Identity" in *New Feminist Discourses: Critical Essays on Theories and Texts,* ed. by Isobel Armstrong (London: Routledge, 1992), 135-153, I am aware of the possible inappropriateness of quoting Cixous in a discussion about a black woman's writing. Kanneh might be right in arguing that the "power of Cixous' metaphors comes precisely from their continuing life in present ideologies of race" (145), but in view of Cixous' inscription of her Jewish identity, her being born just before the Holocaust, and her German mother tongue, I disagree with Kanneh's description of Cixous' "defiant attempts to disengage the specificity of historical metaphor" (145).

15 One of the "texts" in *Eva's Man* describes the poverty of the Canada family, as, for example, when Eva gets yelled at by her mother for peeling the skin of potatoes in too thick slices (27), or when she puts too much grease into the pot (32). The poverty of her family also becomes apparent when they cannot let Alfonso, Jean, and Otis stay with them: "they saw what kind of space we had" (38).

16 Brian McHale focuses his definition of ontology on questions such as "Which world is this? What is to be done in it? Which of my selves is to do it?" and on ontological problems such as the ontology of the

literary text itself and that of the world it projects (10). This focus could certainly be enlarged to include the ontological status of the literary subject and of notions of subjectivity in a postmodernist culture.

17   The issue of how to formulate "the inexpressible," or how to write an unlived, an unformed, or a deformed subjectivity connects the central problem in *Eva's Man* to many recent studies on fictionality. In *S/Z* Roland Barthes returns repeatedly to the grammatological restraint in the French language which allows only a he or a she and has no nomenclature for the castrato. In "The Critical Difference: BartheS/BalZac" Barbara Johnson also argues that "The castrato is simultaneously outside the difference between the sexes as well as representing the literalization of its illusory symmetry," *The Critical Difference* (Baltimore: The Johns Hopkins UP, 1980) 10. See also Elizabeth Meese and Alice Parker, "'Grins . . . without the Cat': Introductory remarks in 'The difference within'," *The Difference Within: Feminism and Critical Theory* (Amsterdam: John Benjamins: 1989) 1-12. Many studies on the female *Bildungsroman* express a similar problem: "the female subject" and "the mature subject" as notions are opposed in the dominant culture. Culturally, historically, linguistically, the mature female subject is inscribed as an oxymoronic entity. Many critical works on the female narrative of *Bildung* focus on how patriarchal structures consistently deform the female subject, casting her in a dependent, secondhand role, forcing upon her structures shaped and accepted by men. In the introduction to her study *Living Stories, Telling Lives,* Joanne S. Frye explains that "Female characters lack autonomy because an autonomous woman is an apparent contradiction in cultural terms" (5). The problem of how to express the "taboo," how to write a still quite unformulated and unformulable female subjectivity remains a most troubling issue for women writers of both races, but for African American female writers the conflict between racial and gender identities often sharpens the issue. To quote Elliott Butler-Evans:

"The representation of race requires its own semiotic strategies, featuring ethnic differences and developing coherent patterns of self-construction. Conversely, because racial discourse, particularly when it stresses opposition, gravitates toward totality, threatening to erase all nuances, it often conflicts with the construction of a female character," *Race, Gender, and Desire: Narrative Strategies in the Fiction of Toni Cade Bambara, Toni Morrison, and Alice Walker* (Philadelphia: Temple UP, 1989) 19. See also Barbara Christian's classic article "Trajectories of Self-Definition: Placing Contemporary Afro-American Women's Fiction," *Black Feminist Criticism: Perspectives on Black Women Writers* (New York: Pergamon, 1987) 171-186.

18   In "On Seduction" Jean Baudrillard opposes a seductive discourse which represents only surface with a discourse of interpretation which "wants to get beyond appearances; this is its illusion and fraud." *Selected Writings*, ed. Mark Poster (Stanford: Stanford UP, 1988) 150.

19   Toni Morrison's gripping essay *Playing in the Dark: Whiteness and the Literary Imagination* (New York: Vintage Books, 1993) shows the degree to which blackness has been central in the writerly versions of whiteness in this country.

20   All the translations from the Swedish are mine.

21   See, for example, *The Voyage In: Fictions of Female Development*, ed. Elizabeth Abel, Marianne Hirsch, and Elizabeth Langland (Hanover: UP of New England, 1983).

4

The Rhetoric of Freedom in
Charles Johnson's *Oxherding Tale* and
Sherley Anne Williams' *Dessa Rose*.

"and yet all were conserved in this process of doubling"
(*Oxherding Tale*)

"The sign of an authentic
voice is thus not self-identity
but self-difference." (Barbara Johnson)

Charles Johnson's *Oxherding Tale* (1982) and Sherley Anne Williams' *Dessa Rose* (1986) are two African American narratives of *Bildung* which describe a journey from slavery to free personhood and, in the process, raise complex questions about freedom. Focusing on one of the most pivotal subject transformations in African American history, these narratives of *Bildung* dialectically explore and attempt to heal the painful rift in the African American subject position. The political, social, and economic forces that worked against the African American people who passed from slavery to free personhood were extreme. Yet, their difficult and complicated position keenly illustrates the double position of all subjects: while they attempt desperately to control their personal subject formation, they are constantly subjected to and controlled by systems that they cannot, for various reasons, escape or dismantle. Maybe for this reason, these novels attempt to destabilize and externalize racial and rhetorical limits that are placed on, in, and around bodies and words. Based on difference rather than on identification, these rhetorical investigations lead to a rather impersonal interpretation of freedom as neither essential nor existential, neither stasis nor struggle. This subtle and sophisticated notion of freedom becomes one of the leading contributions to the formulation of an African American postmodernism and a significant aspect of the African American narrative of *Bildung*.

Many African American authors, including Johnson and Williams, attempt to project a double notion of freedom. First, as they struggle to destabilize the relationship between black and white, they explore the dialogic difference within the rhetoric of both subject and world from an African American perspective. Second, they double the pursuit of material and intellectual freedom with an excavation and an exhibition of rhetorical tropes for race and subjectivity—tropes which tend to stagnate and imprison—in order to liberate the notion of freedom from a rhetorical stasis and to expose sites of cultural blindness. Johnson, for example, underscores the double and dialectic aim by using a syllogistic structure, a structure which he highlights through the three appearances of the mystical and threatening figure called the Soulcatcher. The young protagonist, Andrew, meets the Soulcatcher beside the putrefied and stinking corpse of a runaway slave, beside a nightly fire when the protagonist himself has become a runaway slave, and, at the end of the novel, beside his dead lover, Minty. The Soulcatcher is a professional manhunter of unclear racial origin who takes on the features of his victims and whose victims continue to live as live tattoos on his body. Inscribing change and process, he is the most destabilizing factor of the text. He truly suggests a critique of the binary as he is both black and white; and in addition, he is neither or more. His place of origin is erased. He represents the excess factor, that which does not add up. The striking outcome of this meeting between the run-away slave and the slave hunter is that the Soulcatcher does not kill Andrew; he sets him free. I submit that the Soulcatcher externalizes a rhetoric of the brutal history of African Americans in America and reshapes that rhetoric by destabilizing the limits of traditional symbols and metaphors for blackness. He sees freedom as lack of desire and a turning away from body and language, physicality and textuality, two of the main forces that have kept black people enslaved. His presence also suggests that the African American formulation of future freedom is closely linked to an understanding of the past and has a material base. Johnson recreates the fight for racial, social, and political equality through processes of renaming and redefining. He invests the creation of contemporary versions of historical reality with the hope that fresh perspectives on the past can open new visions of the future. Paradoxically, then, Johnson's historical focus is utopian. In a possibly analogous way, Dessa's pregnant body destabilizes the social and rhetorical structures it inherits. Deborah E. McDowell argues that *Dessa Rose* "links getting 'beyond' slavery to remembering it, paradoxically burying it and bearing it, a process exemplified in the naming of Dessa's baby" (155). Encompassing the parameters of human life—death and birth—both the killer and the pregnant mother become central catalysts for change.

Oxherding Tale describes the African American passage from slavery to free personhood. The story begins at a South Carolina cotton plantation and ends after the Civil War when, with his wife and daughter, the liberated slave Andrew Hawkins wants to rebuild the world. Focusing on a voyage through different spatial locations from Cripplegate to "the world," *Oxherding Tale* reminds the reader of the close etymological relationship between the words *Bildung* and building. In contrast, *Dessa Rose* begins with Dessa's memories of the death of her lover, the father of her unborn child, as she is kept chained in an underground root cellar. Covering a sharply cruel passage from slavery to freedom, Dessa's narrative of *Bildung* ends with her telling her story to her child and hearing him pass it on to his children as if these memories were his own. For Dessa, as for the old woman in invisible man's dream cave, freedom is the right to say what is in your mind, to formulate your own subjectivity and the world as you see it, and to resist internalizing the way others read you. She also struggles to gain possession of her own body, a right which is inseparable from the right to keep one's own children and to stay together as family. Beyond the limits of her own body, however, space threatens Dessa. When it was in her womb she had at least a chance to protect her child, but in the world she has never known any safe spaces. Her use of rhetorical figures such as "the hole in blackness" when her brother is sold away reflects her association of space with pain, separation, and death. Her fear of the spatial dimension leads her to focus her narrative of *Bildung* around the dimension of time as it is expressed through generations, but the focus is on the loss of generations—mother, father, brother, sister—and on the exacting price her generation paid for the relative safety of the younger generations.   Public and private, spatial and time-related, in both *Oxherding Tale* and *Dessa Rose* the pursuit of freedom demands a reconstruction of economic, material, and rhetorical hierarchies.

Tropes for Blackness in *Oxherding Tale*

In Charles Johnson's *Oxherding Tale*, *Bildung* is a process of expulsion. Throughout the book, the focus is invariably on putting liquids and foods into your mouth, into your body. This symbolic language of the internalization of the limits and rules of the slave system is full of horror at the unavoidability of that process, but it is also full of longing for processes of change, purging, and liberation. Vacillating between two foci—body and text—the narrator of *Oxherding Tale* concretizes this longing in a syllogistic structure which is duplicated in the larger map of the novel. Whereas the first part of the novel deals with notions of body and physicality, the second half concentrates on questions about language and textuality.   Johnson introduces this double structure in the first chapter which sets up a dialectic between notions such as body and language, nature and culture, woman and man, and dreams (and memories) of Africa and the reality of America.   The story begins with Andrew Hawkins' reaction to the double influence of his falling in love with a fellow slave, Minty, and his increasing hatred of the white education his master forces upon him. The clash between black and white worlds, between the black girl who makes Andrew dream of Africa and the white culture that only serves to separate him further from his own culture, brings Andrew to rebel and to demand his manumission papers.   His long maturation process, however, takes him from Cripplegate deeper and deeper into physical bondage until he narrowly escapes the mines by passing into the world of whites where his "education" increasingly focuses on the role of language in the race-divided South.   When he marries a white girl, he thinks she possesses a language of stable concepts and he feels translated into an archaic world of meaning. Andrew Hawkins' exposé of the Southern slave system balances the double influence of physical and intellectual bondage and turns finally, through the figure of the Soulcatcher, to a critique of the internalized tropes which identify the races and keep that system intact.

An expressionistic and imaginative author, Charles Johnson is suspicious of realism, naturalism, and so-called factual history. In *Being and Race* (1988) he describes his admiration for such naturalistic precursors as James Baldwin, Richard Wright, and John A. Williams and his attempts to imitate their social realism. His struggle with naturalism taught him that writing is a process that does not imitate experience but that primarily creates experience.

> In hindsight, naturalism seemed to conceal profound prejudices about Being, what a person is, the nature of society, causation, and a worm can of metaphysical questions about what could and could not logically occur in our "experience" and conscious life. Its implied physics was dated—or at best only provisional—and, even worse, it concealed a reductionistic model of human psychology, of what motivates men and women (and had no theory of the self at all), that made my characters dull and predictable in their inner lives and perceptions of the world. Like gravity, it held the imagination close to the ground by creating a camera-like illusion of objectivity, of events unmediated—or untampered with—by any narrative presence. Although easy to imitate as a style, it scaled down experiential possibilities and put curious limits on narrative voice and language, as well as on such poetic devices as simile and metaphor, those inherently existential strategies that allow a writer to pluck similarities from our experiences or to illuminate one object by reference to another by saying A *is* B. (6)

Johnson's ability to turn realism into an imaginative and magic literature resides particularly in his creative use of language and in the manner in which he combines history and art, life and literature. Karl Marx's short visit to Cripplegate is one outstanding example of Johnson's free use of reference and fictionality, which adds to the postmodernist qualities of the novel. The double world of fact and fiction in *Oxherding Tale* also reminds the reader of Linda Hutcheon's definition of postmodernism as "one which juxtaposes and gives equal value to the self-reflexive and the historically grounded: to that which is inward-directed and belongs to the world of art (such as parody) and that which is outward-directed and belongs to 'real life' (such as history)" (1989: 2). It also underscores the double experience of the African American people for whom many "facts" have been and remain pure fiction. Exploring the limits between fact and fiction, Johnson places his subject in a specific historical situation while he openly parodies much of the white Western canon. One of the great strengths in Johnson's novel lies in its ability to confront the reader with his or her notions of race, subjectivity, and genericity from a historical perspective.

The self-reflexive rendition of the historical dimension is crucial to the structuring of the subject in Hawkins' tale. His narrative of *Bildung* describes his struggle to recognize and to create a place for the African American experience in the historical text, and his attempts to change the African American marginalized position and his (and the readers') notions about that position. The lesson he seems to convey is strikingly similar to that of invisible man's grandfather: to live a life totally subjected to history is to live a lie. And Andrew Hawkins feels that he does live a lie, both when he is a slave and when he passes for a white man. He struggles with the realization that history is an infinite net-work of possible subject positions, but that the racial tropes uphold an ethnocentric system which consistently denies African Americans opportunity to "rebuild the world." In *Being and Race* Charles Johnson writes that "The black American writer begins his or her career with—and continues to exhibit—a crisis of identity. If anything, black fiction is *about* the troubled quest for identity and liberty, the agony of social alienation, the longing for a real and at times a mythical home" (8). The home that Andrew Hawkins wants to rebuild at the end of the war (and at the end of the novel) is no less than the world itself. His narrative of *Bildung* takes him from a past of total subjection which is, in his words, "mere parable" and "a lie" through a journey of being and race, of the double texts of body and language, to the typically inconclusive ending of the African American narrative of *Bildung* where text and world finally confront each other.   Even though Johnson's narrative of *Bildung* is historical, it expresses a desire similar to the one found in *Invisible Man*: placing Brechtian limitations on cathartic endings, it fuses into the dimension of the real.   Paradoxically, when Andrew Hawkins' narrative of *Bildung* stops, the story of the world can begin, and this precisely is the capsule of the utopian element in Charles Johnson's novel.   The ethnocentric education Andrew receives at Cripplegate makes him acutely aware of how excluded the reality of slaves are from history and literature.   Even as the name Cripplegate negates itself, it becomes a good description of the place in Andrew's eyes.   On the one hand, the plantation teaches Andrew all the crippling facts of what it is like to be colonized and dispossessed.   On the other hand, it becomes, for Andrew, a gate to a different world.   Subjected to a, for him, useless education in white culture, Andrew begins a revolt, thus starting the process of gaining his own subjective voice.   Polkinghorne may congratulate himself for his liberal spirit when he provides education for the slave boy, but this education produces not the cultivated gentleman-slave that can bring the owner higher profit, but rather a rebellious slave, hungry for his own voice.   When Andrew falls in love with Minty, he gains a sense of direction and reason enough to express his own desire.   When he runs to his master to inform him that he is getting married to Minty and that he wants him to draw up his deed of manumission, it is no less than insurrection.   This dramatic scene between slaveowner and slave, between empty patriarchal gestures and the desperate need for substantial changes, launches Andrew Hawkins' utopian narrative of *Bildung*.

Andrew Hawkins' life begins with an unrecorded accident, one more missing historical record regarding African Americans and the narrator's wish to supply an imaginative complement.   In a drunken attempt by two men to avoid the displeasures of their respective wives, they switch night quarters.   The plantation owner stumbles down to the slave quarters while Andrew's father, so ordered by his owner, climbs the stairs to his mistress' room: "in perfect submission to his Master's will, he turned inside and walked like a man waistdeep in weeds down a hallway where every surface, every shape was warped by frail lamplight from Jonathan's study" (5). Johnson uses metaphoric language with greater abundance than, for example, Gayl Jones in *Eva's Man*. Yet, Johnson too at times uses the double linguistic code of metaphor and metonymy in order to separate the double existence of slave and master, oppressed and oppressor. The description of George Hawkins as he walks toward his master's bedroom is one poignant example. Absorbing all the warping powers of the master and the slave system, the frail light from his master's study is a metonymic image. From the master, to his study, to the light from his study, the transference of features from one end of the preexisting link to the other is complete. Walking through that light, on foreign soil as it were, George feels "like a man waistdeep in weeds." This metaphoric image indicates an exchange of features from two different realms via a third party. The natural image of weeds contradicts the white, ordered, and bourgeois milieu it is supposed to render visual. Thus the metaphor functions to remind the reader of the double perspective that the slave system creates which shows that, although many white men and women grew wealthy and established on the Southern plantations, they like weeds took their livelihood from others. The weed-image is also intricate in how it signifies on the various Southern myths that white men were, by nature and through God, morally superior to black men and therefore destined to control them. The double linguistic code structures the divided world of the slave plantations and functions as a lesson in difference.

Andrew Hawkins, the double subject in *Oxherding Tale*, is the ultimate product of this difference and full of the disruptive energy and lack of closure which commonly follow the sign. His birth is the beginning of the end of tranquillity on the plantation. On a personal level the birth of the boy destroys two marriages. His white mother, Anna Polkinghorne, never forgives her husband, chooses celibacy, and withdraws into mental and physical illness after the birth of the boy. His black stepmother never forgives his father who loses his privileged position as butler and house slave. Sent to work in the fields, George decides that he has been a traitor and a tool for the white oppressor, and he becomes an avid advocate for the race. Growing up in the quarters, his son feels his double birth and finds it hard to emulate George's example. He feels that he belongs to both the black and the white worlds, and he grows up feeling the animosity between them focus on him. Andrew learns that even as he is both a Hawkins and a Polkinghorne, he is neither. His double identity is unacceptable to both families. On a less personal level, the birth of Andrew Hawkins represents the beginning of a kind of synergetic reaction. Before him the division between slaves and slaveowners was intact and unthreatened. His birth signals, however, a transgression of limits, and the beginning of a communication process between races and classes at Cripplegate which results, as any synergetic reaction, in changes to both systems and a mixture that is greater than the sum of the two individual effects. The process of interaction also has an accumulative effect. It marks the beginning of the end of the protected lives of whites at Cripplegate. Anna and Jonathan Polkinghorne shrivel up and have no children to take their place. For Andrew, in contrast, the tear in the system marks a possible opening. He is both signifier, speaker of the new and unnamable, and signified, object of the others' fears and desires.

By singling him out and treating him differently from the other slave children, Andrew's master confirms the doubleness of the boy's background. Fully aware that Andrew is the only child of his own wife, Polkinghorne feels a responsibility for the boy that exceeds caring for property. He hires an instructor to educate Andrew, a strangely excitable fellow named Ezekiel William Sykes-Withers. When he arrives, this tutor asks the slaveowner if the boy he will be in charge of is Polkinghorne's son. He answers no but his gestures say yes. Jonathan Polkinghorne does not have the ability nor the courage to resolve the contradictions of the situation, so he reifies both the slave child and the white cultural education he provides for him. Reinforcing the notion that in an oppressive system no events are unpolitical, devoid of value or neutral, the education Polkinghorne arranges for Andrew is ultimately a crippling opportunity for both. An education which might not be bad in itself, when offered to a child under slavery, becomes one more efficient tool of oppression. On the other hand, for Polkinghorne it also has an unexpected result since

Andrew's sense of alienation and boredom feeds his need to be liberated. Facing the massive force of a white discourse that marginalizes him as unspeakable other, a stereotyped signified, Andrew desires the position of signifier. When gazed upon from the slave quarters, the whole system looks like a lying web of excuses clothing a profitable system of exploitation and appropriation. In order to construct a semiotic field of exchange and of change, Andrew tries to destabilize this system through processes of externalization.

For Andrew Hawkins the cripple-gate is formed by a double influence of education and love. However, since the education he receives is one focused solely on white culture and his love is the love and longing for Africa, the influence of these two forces pulls Andrew in different directions. Both *Oxherding Tale* and *Middle Passage* include a scathing critique of the education that white people provide for African Americans, illustrating the useless distance between a formal classicist training and the historical reality of African American people. In *Middle Passage* Rutherford Calhoun describes the schooling he got from his former owner. "A biblical scholar, he endlessly preached Old Testament virtues to me, and to this very day I remember his tedious disquisitions on Neoplatonism, the evils of nominalism, the genius of Aquinas, and the work of such seers as Jakob Böhme. . . . Since the hour of my manumission . . . I hungered—literally *hungered*—for life in all its shades and hues: I was hooked on sensation, you might say, a lecher for perception and the nerve-knocking thrill, like a shot of opium, of new 'experiences'" (3). Andrew condemns not only the abstract dated quality of the white man's learning, but he also opposes its deadening boredom. The hunger for color and sensual impressions is a constant theme in the African American canon, a theme often reinforced by authors who seek to convey those sensations through the rich texture of their language. Toni Morrison's "funkiness" in *The Bluest Eye* is just one example of the haunting sensuality that African American narrators connect with their longing for Africa.[1] Andrew fares even worse than Rutherford. He has to learn Greek, Latin, monadology, classic philology and Oriental philosophy, Hegel, Thoreau, and Marx, but none of these systems helps Andrew with his daily existence. Lacking everything that is basic to human life, his learning increases his sense of alienation. The abstract and ethnocentric quality of his learning is externalized in the figure of his tutor.

The description of the arrival of Ezekiel illustrates the destabilization process that externalizes limits such as the one between his and his student's reality and the one between reality and textuality. The description begins with the stillness and silence that surrounds the snow covered quarters, family house, forest, and fields. Out of this whiteness, the tutor emerges, but he does not appear all at once. The snow makes it seem as if he appears piece by piece, in metonymic fashion—his fingers, his prayerbook, his coat, his hat. Intimating the white silence of the empty paper followed by the appearance of text, the description of this arrival actually imitates not reality but textuality; it parodies the fragmenting and fusing hermeneutic of the mimetic reading process. It also shows that whiteness, like blackness, is a structure. When Andrew's tutor arrives, he is the only living thing that is not frozen by the winter. The passage contrasts him to nature, implying that he is unnatural. He is also a metonymic and a fragmented figure. Fragmentation of the human subject represents another technique which externalizes the internal and destabilizes the solidity of that subject. In Charles Johnson's novels this process is full of both fear and desire.

Fear and desire are also closely linked when it comes to love. Both Andrew Hawkins and Dessa Rose become fluent in double talk when they fall in love and experience the pleasures of sensuality and sexuality. These are moments when both protagonists reach for metaphors to describe their emotions. When Minty calls him into the barn, Andrew feels as if he sees her for the first time. But what he sees is not only the individual girl that he desires but she comes to represent all women he had ever seen and wanted before. To Andrew, Minty becomes a multiple figure who knows how to contain many bodies in one, how to be both many and one. She has, in other words, the metaphoric quality that Andrew seeks. When he wants to describe the effect she has on him, he becomes lyrical. He describes her eyes, which are green, as the water from the mountains when the snow is melting and he thinks of her as a part of the colorful and sensuous African landscape which has been violently uprooted and transferred to an alien part of the world where it will die. Her name might be of Ethiopian origin, and he thinks about that name as a piece of pottery from the Inca culture. Andrew's extended metaphors about Minty as mountain water and pond water, as African and (native) American illustrate her double situation and foretell her horrible death. Minty dies from pellagra, a disease caused by a deficiency of niacin and protein in the diet. If slavery has reduced Minty to so many parts—black skin, strong back, competent hands—the disease rots her body until it, literally, dissolves into parts. As she is dying Andrew dreams of taking her north, to Boston, to an Eastern beach where they will find colors that would complement Minty's colors, where she could become part of nature and wash herself clean of the stench from the slave markets. His description makes use of metonymies —the stench of petroleum and the marketplace— for the exploitive and reifying slave system and opposes them to the metaphoric qualities of Minty. Andrew's desire for Minty parallels his desire for cultural self-representation. She becomes his symbol, the beginning and ending metaphor; her death then suggests an inherent critique of the symbolic and metaphoric representations of blackness present in Johnson's novel.

As an expression of *Bildung*, *Oxherding Tale* represents an exploration of rhetorical limits and how to transgress and transform them through processes of externalization. The strategies in the text are to render these limits porous, to show how they continuously shift and change, and to exploit these shifts socially, economically, and metaphorically to produce a sense of mobility and liberty. This is particularly true of the color line, the border between slave and non-slave, but even death becomes a limit which can be transgressed and transformed as in the tattoos on the Soulcatcher's body. In the cave dream, invisible man paints the picture of a young black woman pleading with a group of white slaveowners, an image which emphasizes the degree to which the physical body distinguishes an African American from a white American, a man from a woman, and a slave from a free person. But since, at the time Johnson's novel is set, many slaves were quite indistinguishable from their white owners, the power of determining who was and was not a slave did not lie in the actual body of the slave. Rather, white people controlled an intricate system of racial and economic differentiation from which many of them derived great profits.[2] Johnson shows how the reification of bodies and cultures were two forceful aspects of this fine-tuned legal system constructed to exploit black people when he makes his young protagonist begin a series of transgressions as he reevaluates his body and his education. When he demands his deed of manumission, he trembles under a new sense of responsibility and he is awed by the possibility of authenticity. He feels as if he has lived under a tight skin where everything he has—his body, his clothes, his knowledge, his language— was not his to use and alienated himself from himself until he experienced himself as a lie. In Andrew's experience, the slave system has drawn this limit between a false and an authentic subjectivity on and into the body by epidermalizing being. Wanting to find new clothes for his body and giving it a new shape, Andrew plots his escape. His first attempt involves a transference of features from his own body on to the system of slavery. The second half of the novel which deals with his passing into white society illustrates the limitations of this idea, but at the beginning of the novel, Andrew is young and he conceives of the transition from one system to another as a kind of birth, a rejuvenation, a shedding of skin like a snake. This first birth, however, is stillborn: his master suppresses the revolt by simply refusing to draw up Andrew's deed of manumission. But, even though Andrew's first attempt at escaping slavery is a failure, his short moment of insurrection has tested the limits which he had internalized and shown him their instability. Like Ellison's invisible man, Andrew has come to dread the double identity which the system of slavery forces on him. His second step away from it is to escape from the white education which only reinforces his sense of doubleness.

The first part of the novel explores bondage and lies through the physical body as Andrew experiences sexuality, drugs, and labor; the second part focuses on the lies of language as Andrew confronts his longing for eternal identities of being and race. The chapters in the first part focus on different aspects of the body, especially on how it writes itself as symptom. First, it focuses on the relationship between the body and world when Mattie decides that eating meat is a violation of civilization. A symptom of expulsion of all that is evil in the world, vegetarianism shows her perception of the body as a part of that world and how unclear the border between body and world can be. Andrew's tutor supplies another example of how the border around the body shifts and moves. An avid follower of Transcendentalism, the tutor distrusts everything material from his own body to the structures of the world. He lives for his ideological dreams and is, in fact, severely chastised by Karl Marx for his lack of a materialistic base for his argument. Marx, who maintains that truth is someone, asks the tutor if his mother would understand his talk about the transcendental ego. But for all his bookish learning, Ezekiel is a man obsessed with his body. Everything physical entices him. He sleeps in his clothes, women and cripples scare him, and in his room he has dozens of mirrors hung up on the walls and the door. Everywhere he looks, his body—multiplied—is in focus. Johnson is fascinated with the idea of the body as a changeable, multiple, many-faceted object. Both Andrew Hawkins and Rutherford Calhoun in *Middle Passage* confront one body, one physical shape, which contains and can change into a multitude of bodies. In an image of history which is both personal and collective and utopian and material, the Soulcatcher in *Oxherding Tale* and the Allmuseri god in *Middle Passage* present and represent the challenge of the limitless. The inscription of the material sharpens the distinction between limits and the limitless and the subjective possibility of incorporating both.

The focus on bodily differences also inspires commentary on gender differences. Andrew, for example, thinks that men are illiterate in issues of the heart. Whatever Andrew means with "the heart," he suspects that women understand it and thus have a more holistic, intuitive, "feeling," sense of knowledge about the world where men know Being only in the shape of the Periodic Table. He also seems to believe that this difference affects language and grammar. Ezekiel reinforces Andrew's suspicions when he argues that it is hard to be a full-grown man because he believes that, since they have no essential function in the universe, men are weaker than women. They build machines, he argues, have little boy-clubs, and believe that their ideas will perish in history. He suspects that men are caught in diachronic time but that women know eternal and synchronic time. For both Andrew and Ezekiel the bodily differences between men and women are the basis for gender distinctions in relation to truth, time, and history. Both men argue that the body can somehow escape the influence of textualization, yet, both use language metaphorically to express this opinion. Thus, their examples have a synergetic function; the contextual influence or "contamination" between body and language serves to demonstrate the closeness of the two systems and how inseparable our experience of the one is from the other. When Andrew tries to describe Ezekiel's manner of thinking he evokes this doubleness of body and language when he says that his tutor's language was shaped and reshaped "like soft wax" (31).

Andrew soon learns that bodies, too, like language, can be shaped like wax. When he becomes Flo Hatfield's lover, she not only dresses him and intoxicates his body with various drugs, but she also wars relentlessly on his books and his way of speaking. Highly trained in argumentative skills by his former tutor, Andrew soon learns to agree with and to approve of everything that she says. His new skills in listening are a part of this training but the most important lesson he learns is the degree to which language influence bodies and impressions of bodies. Hawkins' eventual passing and survival hinge on this ability to change his body in and through language. When called upon to present official papers or to be sent back into slavery, Hawkins produces a new reconstructed biography, a life story that performs the miraculous transcultural passage, a verbal illusion of freedom and whiteness. This verbal illusion works on the white guard, but it also has power over Hawkins, now a Mr. Harris, which is seen in his desperate desire for stability and for a synchronic interchangeability. When he meets Peggy Undercliff, his future wife, he is primarily attracted to her way of talking and the sense he gets that she has access to a dimension of language where words and meanings do not change. During the wedding ceremony, he feels translated into an older, more archaic and authentic language, which in some ways, in spite of racial and social differences, connects his new woman to Minty, whom he has lost. If Minty externalized Andrew's rhetoric of blackness, Peggy externalizes his rhetoric of whiteness. The white woman brings out Hawkins/Harris' Platonic dream of an essential life which stands in stark contrast to his own life which he sees as puzzle made out of inauthentic pieces, and his personality which he sees as a combination of traits from different quite disparate sources. He has learned to incorporate the division in his life, but he still dreams of a wholeness which his present situation cannot confirm. Even though Minty, Flo, and Peggy have taught him different aspects of language, he still dreams of a freedom outside of language in a realm where textual instability is transformed into eternal meaning. For all his desire to learn from them, the three female teachers seem only to reinforce his sense of alienation and his fear of termination and death. The parallel he has created between body and language still traps him in a nostalgic longing for the archaic and the authentic. It takes the Soulcatcher to shake him out of this constellation.

The Soulcatcher, this mysterious and murderous character who brings both life and death, externalizes the syllogism between body and text since he combines both. The complex issues of how to read and interpret him and the combination of body and text that takes place on his skin full of live tattoos furthers the destabilization of traditional tropes for blackness and whiteness. He stands not as a symbol nor as a metaphor, but as a floating signifier that emphasizes the written, the relative and temporal, nature of all historical "truth." The Soulcatcher contradicts every system. Undermining the possibilities of symbolic and metaphoric truth, he simultaneously illustrates these rhetorical methods as constructions with temporary meaning. The Soulcatcher highlights the traditional racial tropes. There is little doubt that in some ways the Soulcatcher symbolizes the soul of black folks, the essentialist center of blackness rooted in history and folk tradition. Andrew first hears it in the tune of his voice, then sees it in his face. Listening to his twang, Andrew swears that his voice was black. Looking into his face he sees graphic evidence of the genetic mix which he feels is a part of every American. He sees African features and features that remind him of his father. A slavehunter and a killer could be seen as a figure who devours people, but the slavecatcher's mouth is described as only a thin line, a slash, in his face. This description strengthens his position as that which externalizes; he carries his victims on the outside, on the surface of his body. A slave who hunts slaves, he is dressed both as a house slave and a field slave. The Soulcatcher undoes all systems; his professional enterprise overturns the hierarchies of the South, Andrew's sense of order and morale, and the textual systems of signification he illustrates. A mongrel, he is and he is not a symbol of blackness. He establishes and erases the symbolic dimensions of the text which commonly are predestined toward a certain and final truth, and in the flicker of light between truth and untruth he begins to trace a different relationship to the always already soul of black folks. In the economy of the text, the Soulcatcher's function is to capture and critique the inherent limitations of both transcendent, symbolic truth and to immanent, metaphoric truth. Survival, he maintains, lies in learning to unlearn the semiotic traps and to become attuned to new and different structures of signification. When he tells Andrew that he, the Slavecatcher, caught his first black man who was passing for white because of the slave's rhetorical imagery he gives Andrew a clue of the externalizing work that he has to grasp if he wants to remain free.

The presence of the Soulcatcher also captures the collapse of traditional Western categories within this textual system. He is carnivalesque in a Bakhtinian sense—chaotic, anarchistic, intuitive. He is also Manippean—political, cruel, realistic. He explodes the traditional tropes of symbol and metaphor. When he bares his body for Andrew and shows him the multiplicity of live tattoos featuring all the Soulcatcher's victims, he turns the metaphoric inside out, externalizing the internal, making the immanent merely skin-deep. He extricates the metaphoric expression from its baggage of delivering a meaning, of stating a truer truth than the non-metaphoric expression can. Staring at the body of the Soulcatcher, Andrew sees the Soulcatcher's past and his own past; he sees the history of African Americans and the rhetoric it has created. He sees himself and his father and an uncanny dance of physical metamorphoses which has "no purpose beyond the delight."

Not tattooes (sic) at all, I saw, but forms sardined in his contour, creatures
Bannon had killed since childhood . . . . for nothing in the necropolis
he'd filled stood alone, wished to stand alone, had to stand alone, and the
commonwealth of the dead shape-shifted on his chest, his full belly, his fat
shoulders, traded hand for claw, feet for hooves, legs for wings, their
metamorphosis having no purpose beyond the delight the universe took in
diversity for its own sake, the proliferation of beauty, and yet all were
conserved in this process of doubling, nothing was lost in the masquerade,
the cosmic costume ball, where behind every different mask at the party—
behind snout beak nose and blossom—the selfsame face was uncovered at
midnight, and this was my father, appearing briefly in the dead boy Moon
as he gave Flo Hatfield a goodly stroke and, at the instant of convulsive
orgasm, opened his mouth as wide as that of the dying steer Bannon slew in
his teens, was that steer, then several others, and I lost his figure in this
field of energy, where the profound mystery of the One and the Many gave
me back my father again and again, his love, in every being from
grubworms to giant sumacs, for these too were my father and, in the final
face I saw in the Soulcatcher, which shook tears from me—my own face,
for he had duplicated portions of me during the early days of the hunt—I
was my father's father, and he my child. (175-6)

This synergetic skin-circus concludes the externalization of the racial
tropes and gives Andrew a liberating perspective of his own desire. All his
life, he has been seeking and duplicating an internal and synchronic space
where meaning is eternally anchored and words unchangeably authentic.
This is the space he experienced in Flo Hatfield's house where there was
no outside, no temperature changes, no time, no history, no memory, no
motion. This is a place where language seizes to exist. It was the life he
desired with his wife. It is the part of himself where he has encapsulated
the image of his father who, like his son, is the one with the mouth, the
one who has internalized everything and everybody. Confronted with this
vision on the Soulcatcher's body, Andrew reaches a distance to and a
perspective on himself. The shifting rich mosaic of the Soulcatcher's

necropolis makes Andrew grasp how deeply his longing for the synchronic is a product of the slave-system, and how efficiently it has excluded him from the world. The externalization of his inner landscape frees his longing for that inner space and allows him to enter a historical and diachronic dimension free from desire and from stagnating racial tropes. Liberated from dead and static images of race and subjectivity, he becomes, like Reb, a man without appetite who "can't be caught, he's *already* free" (173). This carnivalesque, material, and rhetorical freedom concludes the process of externalization which is Andrew Hawkins' narrative of *Bildung*.

Blood, Tropes, and Freedom in *Dessa Rose*

Sherley Anne Williams' *Dessa Rose* also focuses on the liberation of the subject, the utopian element in the act of remembrance, the dialectic of a syllogistic structure, and the transformation of racial tropes. Finally free in mind and body, Dessa tells the story of her transition from an ignorant fieldhand to an accomplished social being who masquerades both her pain and her laughter; the syllogism stretches over the separated worlds of blacks and whites in the slave-dependent Southern states and indicates, as does *Oxherding Tale*, that once the practical transgression between the races is initiated, the result is a synergetic explosion of both power and love relationships. Limited in experience and exposure, Dessa trusts her feelings, but these feelings tend to stabilize and stagnate her world into easily separated black and white, good and bad, dichotomies. Her image of the color-divided world is seemingly simplistic, but it reveals the complicated structure of internalized racial tropes. On the one hand, she loves and trusts black people, while she hates and distrusts white people. On the other hand, her metaphors often reveal a *via negativa* of the relationship: a black person is an insect crawling in the face of the white people, a fly in the master's milk. Dessa has internalized the tropes of slavery; her narrative of *Bildung* traces her attempts to liberate herself not only from physical bondage but from its intellectual and emotional bondage as well. She must grasp that the rhetoric of her emotions is learned, not given; it is relative, not absolute; it is temporary, not fixed. In order to explore and explode her lack of freedom, she confronts many of the images which alternatively idealize or denigrate blackness. For Dessa, maturation and liberation come with her understanding that there is "Something that don't have to be real to be true" (249). This realization frees her to understand the value of money compared to physical and "real" commodities such as land and slaves; it permits her to participate in the carnivalesque parody of the Southern system with which the novel ends, beating it at its own game; and finally, it allows her to accept Ruth as a person and to love her even though she is a white mistress who has a black lover. Dessa's African American narrative of *Bildung* concludes with a family portrait out West in a geography free of slavery's bloodstain and her wish to tell her tale, to represent herself, her people, and to convey also her rhetorical struggle for liberation.[3] Her conclusion is a beginning of a new phase, a new historical situation, a new subjectivity, and a new language where the tropes for blackness and whiteness no longer necessarily bind each other into stabilized identities of slave and master.

The Soulcatcher in *Oxherding Tale* announces that in order to catch a runaway slave, that slave must have internalized remnants of the dead and deadly slave system and labor under the burden of a dead desire; the dead system must have contaminated a part of the subject, death must be present inside the slave and make him willing to give himself up for death. Slavery must shackle the slave internally as well as externally. For the slave the only way to maintain any free distance from that system is to be free from desire, to have no image of selfhood other than as slave, and to live without a dream of change. Therefore, both *Dessa Rose* and *Oxherding Tale* present love as the most dangerous force that opposes the slave system. Love, physical and emotional attraction, causes the slave to remember his or her suppressed desires of selfhood. Subversive and powerful, the image of love that Johnson and Williams project has little affinity with a private, limited, or well-contained experience. The consequences of Dessa's and Kaine's feelings for each other threaten to erode the whole system and has a synergetic effect on everybody. It causes the bloody circumstances—the killing of Kaine and Dessa's insurrection—that launch Dessa's narrative of *Bildung* and her voyage toward what she calls her second birth.

The structural syllogism of *Dessa Rose* echoes the historical Middle Passage from a black world to a white world to a world where Dessa can begin the project to dissolve the ruling tropes of race and "de-epidermalize her being." Both Dessa's love for Kaine and the dream of freedom he gives her are connected to a desire for blackness and for Africa. Kaine was born an African American, but he is a musician who learned how to make and string a banjo and how to play it from a saltwater slave, an African. Dessa explains to Adam Nemi that when Kaine first heard this man play the banjo he was playing music from Africa, and it seemed to Kaine that the music spoke straight to him in a way that needed no interpretation. The African man gives Kaine a vision of a homeland where there are no white people, where black people rule themselves and speak languages which are untainted by an oppressive social system. This vision of Africa as a place without white people becomes a major part of Dessa's dream of freedom. When Nemi asks her what she thinks about freedom she answers that she thinks it must be a place without white people.

Dessa's dream about the absent island of Haiti as a place without white people expresses her desire to escape the historical, economic, and rhetorical domination by white people. Yet, Haiti is an absent place in her discourse, locating a hearsay possibility as distant as "Africa." For Dessa and Harker Haiti becomes a symbol and a metaphor for freedom, a trope for the reversal of the Middle Passage, but one they dare not translate into reality. In order to reach Haiti, they would have to entrust their bodies to ships owned by white people, and to put themselves again under the power and authority of white men. Since they have never met a white man who would not immediately assume his right to master them, they turn west instead of east across the waters that separate the free island and their colonialized lives in the American South. But before they go west, Dessa has to confront the tropes which control her sense of personal and racial destiny, her history, her economy, and her language. Dessa's narrative of *Bildung* describes her second birth and the confrontation of stagnant racial images which slavery has produced, particularly of black and white women, and her slow liberation from the internalized codes of racism and sexism.

Dessa's middle passage and second birth is a birth into whiteness. Searching for a place of and a trope for freedom, expecting both to be black, Dessa must instead confront the bloody history of slavery in America and her inability to separate her associations of white people with the spilled blood of black people. Dessa cannot distinguish white from red. Like the preacher in invisible man's cave, she identifies race-relations with the spilling of blood. For the preacher in *Invisible Man* black is red, but for Dessa white is red. She finds that as she has freed herself from the physical shackles of slavery and birthed her firstborn son a free child, she is still entangled in the tropes of race that slavery produces. She has no learning, no education; all she knows is the limited and limiting experiences from the plantation where she was a slave. Nothing in her background has prepared her for the white woman, Rufel or Miz Ruint, she encounters while recovering from her experiences of violence and childbirth. She expresses her hate and fear of white people's power through her distaste of the white woman's red hair and lips. The first time she looks at her Dessa thinks that the white person's red hair looks like fire and that her mouth was a bloody wound across the milkwhite face. Her experiences of the woman are short, in between her dreams of home, but each time she associates white with red, fear with blood. When Dessa wakes up in the white woman's arms she feels caught in a web of red hair and, at times, Dessa has the sensation that she is drowning and that this web makes it impossible for her to move. Her memories of pain and blood from giving birth are also connected to the white woman's red mouth that appears like a gash in the white face. The passage suggests the close-knit and palimpsestic nature of Dessa's associations as the wounds of slavery and of childbirth combine and the pain from the one experience bleeds into the pain from the other, mixing with the blood that trickles from Dessa's spent body onto the white sheets. Dessa's death and resurrection are drawn in blood, and the blood on the sheet shows her that in order to overcome her fear of the mouth in the white face, she must regurgitate or externalize the rhetoric of race that she has learned.

Even though racial differences distinguish the black woman's reactions to blood from those of the white woman, the gendered blood of menstruations and childbirth also binds the women together. Ruled by a sense of powerlessness and isolation, Rufel rarely involves herself actively in matters of the farm or the lives of the black people there. But when she sees and hears Dessa's little newborn baby, she feels, finally, presented with an opportunity to do something. The tiny baby covered in blood needs her and she cleans, dresses, and feeds the baby without hesitation, but when she suddenly sees the brown baby body at her white breast she feels guilty and ashamed. Brought up to be a passive decoration in a man's house, Rufel commonly decides nothing, but a newly-become mother, in the face of a baby's needs, she acts instinctively. The text does not reveal if her feelings of shame stem from her being unused to agency and presence or from, in the Southern historical climate, the inappropriate reversal of roles. Blood binds and divides the white and the black woman as they negotiate space and freedom over the young boy's body. Both women have lost their families and friends, and they both need each other desperately. The blood on the sheet and the blood on the newborn's body signify the fundamental and shared experience of women of all races. Dessa's blood which stains the white bedsheets in Rufel's bed initiates the transgression over the Southern colorlines and the ensuing synergetic contact between the two women and their separate cultures.

The two women's battle over an absent figure they both refer to as "Mammy" becomes a battle over cultural domination and the right to cultural self-representation. It also represents their need to externalize and transform a kind of referentiality which keeps each of them distant from the other. The absent "Mammy" is a signifier without a signified and signals the passage from symbolic and metaphoric representations to semiotic readings of race, from transcendental and essential "truths" of blackness and whiteness to non-essential temporary positions based on difference. This transition initiates a new language which the two women can share and which allows them to individualize each other.   Their struggle over "Mammy" externalizes their rhetoric of race.

Rufel's "Mammy" is a symbolic Uncle Tom figure representing devotion, and white people's blindness to the inhumanity of the slave system.   Rufel uses "Mammy" to lend a kind of transcendental credence to the systematic exploitation of black people.   Her "Mammy" is the well-pressed, well-preserved, well-dressed mother-figure whose image allows Rufel to retain patriarchal and patronizing myths about slavery.   Rufel's "Mammy," who has been to France, is actually more cultivated than any of the white families in Charleston; she reverses the myth of how slavery "cultivates" a "primitive" people.   Rufel's "Mammy" incarnates what Michele Wallace terms "the negative/positive images" of blacks in cultural production.   In Rufel's worldview "Mammy" is the reversal of "the widespread conviction that blacks are morally and/or intellectually inferior" (Wallace 1).   Rufel feels magnanimous toward her image of "Mammy" as somebody who is her superior in knowing how to dress, and she cannot fathom the inherent racism of her attitude.   By turning her dead "Mammy" into a symbol of friendship, she uses the black woman as a "transcendent shield," which shields her from the material and economic realities behind their relationship.   Confronting her illusions of blood relations (and the impossible oxymoronic qualities of a transcendent shield) Rufel begins her process of *Bildung* in African American double consciousness as well as in material and economic matters.

Dispossessed and exploited, Dessa constructs no symbolic metatexts about the slave system.   In contrast to Rufel, who needs to rationalize her position as mistress, Dessa has a desperate need to give her "Mammy" enough strength to protect her children.   In her dreams Dessa struggles with her desire to make her mother powerful and with her knowledge of her mother's impotence in the face of the white master.   Whereas Rufel's construction of "Mammy" represents the power to make a powerless figure powerful through imaginary leaps, Dessa's "Mammy" represents Dessa's desperate need to render the ultimately powerless woman powerful, to give her "Mammy" the authority to interpret.   In her dream Dessa asks her mother, who sits, like Sibyl, on a three-legged stool, to interpret the dream of whiteness that Dessa has had.   Paradoxically, Dessa's dream of whiteness, is no dream.   The power she wants her mother to have is undercut by the repetitive insistence of the missing people: her father killed, the dead children, Jeeter sold away, Dessa sold away.   Because she is, ultimately, a powerless figure, Dessa's "Mammy" cannot have a symbolic or transcendent meaning for Dessa, who knows only too well that material circumstances undercut the symbolic power.   She wants "Mammy" to have a proper name.   The fight for naming "Mammy" exemplifies the conflict between Rufel and Dessa over cultural self-representation, and for the black woman it is a fight against cultural domination.   She expresses her "Mammy's" beauty and blackness in a rhetoric of desire which is metaphoric.

> "What was her name then?" Dessa taunted. "Child don't even know
> its own mammy's name. What was mammy's name? What—"
> "Mammy," the white woman yelled. "That was her name."
> "Her name was Rose."   Dessa shouted back, struggling to sit up.
> "That's a flower so red it look black. When mammy was a girl they named
> her that count of her skin—smooth black, and they teased her bout her
> breath cause she worked around the dairy; said it smelled like cow milk and
> her mouth was slick as butter, her kiss tangy as clabber."
> "You are lying," the white woman said coldly; she was shaking with
> fury. "Liar!" she hissed. (125-26)

Seen from the white culture's narcissistic images of self and other, the white woman's "Mammy" is a good ear, a helpful hand, a reliable mirror in which to see a pleasing self-image, a symbol of the transcendence of the very system it corroborates.   From the perspective of a black culture which attempts to resist the internalization of colonization, "Mammy" represents the desire for an inner, essential being, the memory of Africa and the value of all things black.   Therefore, Dessa makes her into a metaphor, transforms her into a rose of blackness seen against the whiteness of milk. In the economy of the text both symbol and metaphor have limitations and the inherent dichotomy between the two rhetorical figures mainly functions to keep the racial tropes of slavery intact. The confrontation between the two women over the right to name and represent "Mammy" functions as a liberation process which produces "Mammy" as a semiotic sign. This sign is in a sense meaningless; it has no transcendent or immanent truth value. It escapes both the white and the black woman's need for a symbolic or a metaphoric history, and it consequently frees the women from their constructed genealogies.

The black and the white women share a female sense of blood as a creative sign and an attachment to and ensuing transformation of the "Mammy" figure, but the one thing that eventually binds them together in their pranks against the Southern slave system is their complete and systematic exclusion from the material economy. Freedom from history and the tropes of slavery means little in comparison to the material dependency that, although to different degrees, keeps both slaves and white women oppressed. In a successful attempt to reverse that oppression, the two women and a handful of the blacks from the farm begin their exploitation of the Southern system, turning their bloody history into a masquerade of deceit. But traces of Dessa's ambivalence for this kind of freedom remains in her rhetoric. She claims that this "wasn't a nice trick but it was what slavery taught a lot of people: to take everybody so you didn't get took yourself" (228).

> We laughed so we wouldn't cry; we was seeing ourselfs as we had been and seeing the thing that had made us. Only way we could defend ouselves was by making it into some hair-raising story or a joke. (228)

Turning the slave economy into a profitable game, Dessa learns a liberating double perspective; seeing both the slave and the economic system that reifies the slave as object-positions, Dessa continues her liberation from the internalization of slavery. Making herself an object, she paradoxically strengthens her subject position and her sense of freedom.

Dessa's inner sense of freedom is fragile and exposed to the material laws of the South. When she runs into Adam Nemi who takes her to the police office, she can measure the strength and weakness of a private and female freedom. Reversing an exploitive system to her own advantage she feels that she has become free, but the events in the prison quickly teach her the limitations of this freedom. When the white sheriff tells her that she is in jail and not at a carnival he marks the limits to the black woman's joke on the South. Both the sheriff and Adam Nemi take for granted their right to name and to reproduce the other—woman, slave, Negro—in self-flattering ways, and they are certain that only another white man can threaten the order of their universe in a town aptly named "Arcopolis." *Oxherding Tale* ends with an image of the necropolis; the tattoos on the Soulcatcher's body show both the carnage during slavery and after the Civil War. The burlesque exploitation of the South in *Dessa Rose* ends in Arcopolis and includes a scathing critique of the "arche" as white and male (Greek for leader and beginning truth) as the three women in the prison, Dessa, Chole, and Rufel, quickly inscribe their power to undermine the white men's authority.[4] Dessa has already severely shaken Nemi's faith in this white, male narcissistic myth, and he attempts to convey his fears to the sheriff when he tries to stop the sheriff from letting a black woman search another black woman. Because she dissolves his ideas of male rationality and of womanhood, Dessa represents evil to Nemi. The threat that she poses to him stems from the fact that Nemi constructs his male identity as opposed to what he sees as female and black and, therefore, Dessa also threatens his manhood. Nemi's slow realization in the prison that the white woman will lie for Dessa's safety makes him identify all women as the ultimate threat to him, to his science and his research. While the two women and the child are leaving the prison, Nemi, still on his knees attempting to reassemble his book, gives his final judgment that all women are sluts.

Nemi's reconstructing of the negative other to include both black and white women is symptomatic also of the two women's synergetic transgression of the Southern racial categories. After the episode in the prison, the two women learn each other's proper names. Their shared experiences have brought them to a realization of the lack of referentiality behind concepts of blackness and womanhood. Dessa's African American narrative of *Bildung* ends then with a vision of freedom that resembles the one in *Oxherding Tale* and *Invisible Man*. A double life, even when it is profitable, is a product of the slave system and feeds on the racial tropes that slavery produces. As an alternative, Dessa constructs her freedom, her future, and her sense of self as anti-personal, anti-male, and anti-rhetorical. The novel ends with a scene which emphasizes the close relationship between material and rhetorical freedom in the text. Braiding the hair of her friends and grandchildren in the traditional ways of black women, Dessa makes a gesture which inscribes culture and tradition in a material way. At the same time, she tells her story and demonstrates her hard-won rhetorical freedom which fuses the past and the future, restores the memory of the lost generations, and marks her coming to terms with doubleness.

NOTES

1   In describing the young black women who come from Mobile, Aiken, Meridian Toni Morrison writes in *The Bluest Eye*: "They go to land-grant colleges, normal schools, and learn how to do the white man's work with refinement: home economics to prepare his food; teacher education to instruct black children in obedience; music to soothe the weary master and entertain his blunted soul. Here they learn the rest of the lesson begun in those soft houses with porch swings and pots of bleeding heart: how to behave. The careful development of thrift, patience, high morals, and good manners. In short, how to get rid of the funkiness. The dreadful funkiness of passion, the funkiness of nature, the funkiness of the wide range of human emotions" (68).

2   Robert William Fogel and Stanley L. Engerman convincingly describe the profitable nature of slavery in *Time on the Cross* (New York: Norton, 1974).

3   The intricate issue of the parallel between the whip-scarred text on Dessa's body and the white male text that reduces Dessa to a "Darky" has been poignantly discussed by Mae Gwendolyn Henderson in "Speaking in Tongues: Dialogics, Dialectics, and the Black Woman Writer's Literary Tradition," *Changing our own Words: Essays on Criticism, Theory, and Writing by Black Women* ed. Cheryl A. Wall (New Brunswick: Rutgers UP, 1989) 16-37; and Deborah E. McDowell, "Negotiating between Tenses: Witnessing Slavery after Freedom—*Dessa Rose*," *Slavery and the Literary Imagination*, ed. Deborah E. McDowell and Arnold Rampersad (Baltimore: The Johns Hopkins UP, 1989) 144-163.

4   In the suggestive name Arcopolis Williams brings together many meanings in the Greek, such as the various Greek prefixes Arko- (to be enough, to suffice), Arceo- (1. to ward off; 2. to assist, aid, be of use, be strong), Arche- (prefix from Archo; also meaning

beginning, start, principle, authority), Archo- (1. time, to begin; 2. place, to rule, to be the leader of; 3. to be ruled or governed) as well as the word Archon (chief, lord, prince) and Archeon (archives, record).

Conclusion
REpresentation/PREsentation:
Writing the Subject

> What emerges is not a filled subject,
> but an anonymous (nameless) voice
> issuing from the black (w)hole.
> (Baker, *Blues)*

Once upon a time Karl Marx and Stephen Dedalus wanted to wake up from the nightmare which was history. But in African American literature the subject of history is often pursued as an object of desire, even though the history of the African American people is a long tortuous tale of systematic brutalization, reification, and enslavement. This subject radiates the strength and capability of a people who have survived unspeakable and often untold horrors. It also expresses a desire for difference and authenticity. The subject in African American literature has become a highly visible space where this struggle for difference and authenticity is taking place. This arena makes writing and studying the subject a complex task because when the authentic voice gets rooted in history it tends to take on flesh; it needs a body and, once it has a body, it becomes human, it becomes Being in Time. This pursuit of body and being must be viewed in the context of the American slave-system which effectively denied both. Yet, once the subject attracts body and being, it easily becomes not the unreal thing—writing—but the real thing: a victim of referentiality. This I think is the main reason why writing the subject of history appears to temporarily slow down or even close down the poststructural slide. While the interest in the minority subject expresses a desire for difference, it simultaneously shows that this is also a desire for its opposite, a desire for identification, identity, a desire to belong, and to cancel out the difference within a group or a community.

Writing the subject also serves as a help to memory. The more this information age bombards us with data, facts, and computerized number sheets, the more general the state of amnesia seems to get. All over the world, the facts of history are altered to serve the current masters in their fight for power, and few people can make themselves heard over the dim of the information machines long enough to register any resistance at all. There are, of course, a few notable and brave exceptions of authors and writers, most of whom present their versions of events in exile. Aleksandr Solzhenitsyn, Milan Kundera, and Salman Rushdie, to mention a few names, have all put themselves in danger to record memories of political upheavals which the state has wanted to erase from history. Other authors, such as Isaac Bashevis Singer, have labored to evoke the details and flavors of worlds, peoples, and cultures destroyed. But many minorities struggling to maintain a sense of identity different from that which surrounds and threaten to overwhelm them have no access to, or living memory of, a time or a place when and where their culture was unthreatened. And where such records and documents actually did exist, they were frequently systematically destroyed. Therefore, the inscription of history in minority discourse takes on a very special urgency because, as impossible as the task of creating a sense of history is, it is absolutely necessary in order to maintain a sense of hope for cultural survival. Thus, once more, the lingering feeling of desire for history.

The amorous pursuit of the subject that represents history is not totally new. It is also present in Mikhail M. Bakhtin's notion of the chronotope. He called the subject that represents history the artistic "chronotope," a word which literally means "time space." "A literary work's artistic unity in relationship to an actual reality is defined by its chronotope" writes Bakhtin (1981: 243). In Bakhtin's usage, the notion of the chronotope stands out from other more formal devices because it links art and history, and he seems to suggest that the main literary chronotope is man. Or capitalized Man. Even Bakhtin's description of the chronotope acquires a certain anthropomorphic quality when he argues that time "thickens, takes on flesh, becomes artistically visible" and that space "becomes charged and responsive to the movements of time, plot and history" (1981: 84). So it seems that in some ways Bakhtin's view of the chronotope—this visible body that takes on flesh and becomes charged and responsive—was also an object or a subject of desire. But this capitalized Man is in a strange way also ahistorical. He is the product of humanism; gaining most of his strength from excluding others, this universal representative of humankind really only represented a humanity limited to himself. In contrast to this Western tradition, much minority literature pursues chronotopes other than man and inscribes history for other reasons than a nostalgic longing for an Edenic past when Man was absolutely godlike (at least in his own eyes).

The abdication of Man (white, male, Western) as the central literary chronotope has, paradoxically, brought forth the current explosive interest in both minority and postmodernist subjectivity. The subject in African American literature often produces the opposite of the eternal subject in Western discourse; it is the writerly version of history, the subject of history in written form. Its score is temporary. Its beat is syncopated. It listens to a different scale. Noting the constant process of change and the Heizenbergian impossibility to capture both position and movement, it follows the blue notes. One of its pyrotechnical stunts is that it can turn the nostalgic perspective of the past into a utopic vision as we have seen, for example, in the underground image which links slavery and freedom. In a possibly analogous way, the examination of the past serves as a preparation to confront the future and it often takes place at the expense of the Western text; it coincides with the closure of the book. Invisible man, for example, leaves both the underground, his old skin, and his past perspective behind; a disembodied voice, he wishes to speak for everybody in the future. Andrew Hodges in Charles Johnson's *Oxherding Tale* ends that story at the moment when he is free to begin rebuilding the world. Much has been said about the ambiguous endings of African American novels, its parallel to the open-ended structure of the jazz-chord, but these ambiguous closings are clearly anti-Aristotelian; they include a critique of Western ways of structuring subjective experience and meaning.

Writing the subject as a subject of history gives it a sense of ancestry and authenticates the struggle for voice and perspective. This archaeological search for forefathers and foremothers produces a vitally different view of history in African American literature from the one that Stephen Dedalus dreaded or that Milan Kundera describes as "the *wheel of history."* In *The Joke,* for example, one of his characters describes the young Communists as intoxicated because they believed that they were "inaugurating a human era into which man (all men) would be neither *outside* history, nor *under the heel of history,* but would create and direct it" (71). As the title indicates, the joke is on their idealism. We could call this "the bulldozer view" of history; confronted with Auschwitz and Gulag, it commemorates the disappearance and destruction of millions. In African American literature, however, there is commonly a firm resistance to this view of history. Invisible man's grandfather tells his grandson that to live a life totally subjected to history is to live a lie. The story of history is much more useful when seen as what Jean Toomer calls "the root-life of a withered people" (*Cane* 56). In this view, history is a source for cultural and personal replenishment, inspiration, and creativity. This view of history often reaches back into a time that predates the wheels of history that has created the current state of affairs and which gives little reason for hope, in order to find the strength to create an alternative future where the balkanization of cultures does not have to lead to bloodshed. This separation of history from history is exemplary. Writing the subject of African American literature is a process that creates its writerly shape and authentic voice through a series of textual separations which structures its difference.

One major task of the authentic subject of history is to rescue the self from the self. *Invisible Man* has repeatedly been called a *Bildungsroman,* yet, invisible man may be searching not so much for his own identity as for the identity of the blackness that defines him. This blackness, he maintains, does not simply belong either to structure, his skin color, this "accident to the epidermis" or to history. It is the writerly versions of his blackness that he needs to dismantle, and in order to do so he must confront the history of the production of blackness and whiteness. In African American literature this review often takes a spatial shape as exemplified by invisible man's cave-image.[1] In August Wilson's *Joe Turner's Come and Gone* Bynum describes his confrontation with the past as walking around the bend in a road. The ocean of the Middle Passage is probably the most common place to arrive to in African American literature. Loomis, in the same play, describes his meeting with the bones people: "I come to this place . . . to this water that was bigger than the whole world. And I looked out . . . and I seen these bones rise up out the water. Rise up and begin to walk on top of it" (250). When the waves wash the bones up on land, they have flesh and skin and they are black.[2] In Paule Marshall's *The Chosen Place, the Timeless People* some of the characters live close to the ocean and they ask "the reason for its angry unceasing lament. What, whom did it mourn? Why did it continue the wake all this time, shamelessly filling the air with the indecent wailing of a hired mute? Who were its dead?" (362). This spatialization of history strongly suggests that the distance and the desire to approach one's history is equally vital for each new generation of African Americans.

The spatialized historiography is part of a struggle to rescue the past from the past, to save it from the already-read text of the past; it is a weapon in the struggle to defamiliarize the well-known and to rescue it from cliché, blindness, and habit. There are many strategies to do so. One effective strategy is to compress time and make past and present events grow into each other. Toni Morrison uses this strategy in *Beloved* when the baby Beloved describes her attachment to her mother and the voyage during the Middle Passage. "All of it is now   it is always now there will never be a time when I am not crouching and watching others who are crouching too . . . the men without skin bring us their morning water to drink . . . if we had more to drink we would make tears . . . we are all trying to leave our bodies behind . . I cannot fall because there is no room to" (210-213). Beloved tells of the death of her mother from drowning and her own waiting standing in the rain until she comes up and finds Sethe's house. The anger and sorrow over the losses in the past have not diminished because it is all now. Passages such as the one from *Beloved* show that in African American literature the individual perspective also blends with the representational; history is communal.

Writing the subject, other authors have tried to rescue the personal perspective from the impersonality of history. "Dig where you stand" was a popular political slogan when I grew up. The personal and local perspective was expected to be the most efficient path toward general political insight and radical change. It has also been a popular method in the women's movement which advocated that the personal is political. When for example Susan Rubin Suleiman argues for the mother as the subject in the theory of the avant-garde, she turns to her own situation as a mother to explain what she means. "Although I will not claim that mothers live most intimately with disorder and clutter, I do believe that a mother knows internal division and double allegiance as a daily experience; and if she has borne a child, she knows these as a bodily experience as well" (1990: xvii). Because all mothers are supposed to be the guardians of the left-overs (the trash, the babies, the half-eaten sandwiches, the decapitated dolls), the mother-trope could easily be central in a postmodernist paradigm as well. One of the main tasks has been to rescue the female body from the Female Body as it has been reproduced by capitalized Man for centuries and to give that body an authentic voice. Tired of little mermaids who have had to give up their voices in order to tame the animal parts of the lower body, to find a suitable boy to marry, and to win approval from patriarchal daddy, feminists have tried to inscribe the authentic voice *through* the body. But many found themselves come up against such strong cultural taboos that the voice they created sounded almost mad.

"Who dares to speak like God?" asks Hélène Cixous who describes herself as a little mouse in the pocket of God who was "an elegant and maternal young man" (1991: 17). And which God shall we turn to? Is the authentic subject Appolonian or Dionysian? Writing the subject through the body, Cixous refuses to make such a choice. One can also think of texts such as Jacques Derrida's *Glas* or Julia Kristeva's "Stabat Mater" where the very division of the page into three or two parallel texts forces the reader to perform the unthinkable, to break the linear, and to attempt to produce the doubleness of passion and reason, body and mind synthetically yet divided. Apollo and Dionysius, body and mind, critical reason and creative intuition, sameness and difference. Parasitically, the two sides nourish and shape each other in a process that is both self-contradictory and self-erasing. *Difference*, writes Derrida, "does not simply belong either to history or to structure" (1978: 28). It does not simply belong either to life or to death, to meaning or to system. And, we might add agreeing with invisible man, neither does blackness.

Writing of the subject through the body takes on added vibrations in African American literature where writerly versions of the black body, male and female, may very well constitute one of the main literary chronotopes. Toni Morrison highlights it, for example, through Sula's birthmark, Pilate's absent naval in *Song of Solomon*, as well as the whip-scarred body of Sethe and the ghostlike pattern of absence and presence of Beloved in the novel with that name. Charles Johnson also tries to illuminate that blackness as body and text are intricately linked and that physicality and textuality are the two main forces which have enslaved black people. In all his novels bodies are in various ways multiplied, hacked to pieces, or torn apart by disease. One of his most fantastic creations is the character called the Soulcatcher in *Oxherding Tale* who is as reversible as the sign itself—flickering between past and future, black and white, destruction and creation—and trailed by the ambiguity of closure and the indeterminacy which tend to follow the sign. He is a good example of the chronotopic subject. The Soulcatcher externalizes the historical syllogism in the novel and opens a critique of the traditional tropes for blackness. Fraught with danger and promise, silence and stories, the Soulcatcher's body could be a model for the creative and scholarly search for the writing of the subject in African American literature. The series of textual and cultural separations of history from history, self from self, body from body which I have reviewed shows that the recognition of history and ethnic identity is a necessary part of the search for the subject but, to become a constructive tool, it must be accompanied by a poststructural distancing from the very notion of identity as it has been essentialized in Western discourse. R. Radhakrisnan has suggested that it is this combined effort to simultaneously establish and dismantle the subject that marks this unique moment in minority discourse (50).

The doubleness that is characteristic of the writing of the subject in African American literature shows a sophisticated awareness of any text's ability to create and undermine centers within itself. It suggests a notion of excess, an element of overflow, and something that cannot be contained. The inscription of doubleness, the lack of origin and *telos*, and the lack of a sense of progression and stable hierarchies affect the possibilities of completeness, wholeness, coherence, and identities in decisively non-Hegelian ways. This notion of doubleness shatters the subject and can disintegrate bodies. The double subject which is, to use Ferdinand de Saussure's semiotic sign as a model, both a subjectifier and a subjectified produces the narrative of *Bildung* as desire and abhorrence, as identification and difference, as a tension between two halves of the subject and, at times, as a dialogue with the abject.[3] The desire to heal the rift lingers in the writing of the subject, but it is also a desire for closure and for death. When the two halves of the subject either merge or break apart, the desire evaporates, the tension abates, the dialogue becomes silent, and the story ends. There is, in other words, a connection between the double subject and the possibility for a story. This connection might explain in part why the endings of African American narratives of *Bildung* often are ambivalent. It may also express an inherent critique of textual structures which, in order to write the subject in African American literature, must be dramatically transformed.

In the preceding chapters I focused on various aspects of the doubling processes in Ralph Ellison's *Invisible Man*, Toni Morrison's *The Bluest Eye*, Gayl Jones' *Eva's Man*, Charles Johnson's *Oxherding Tale*, and Sherley Anne Williams' *Dessa Rose*. These aspects of doubling are: the double subject which breaks into a subjectifier and a subjectified, pursuing both a personal and a representational history; the double discourse of modernism and postmodernism; the double heritage of black and white literature; the double linguistic code of metaphor and metonymy; the doubling of art and history; the dialectic of material circumstances and rhetorical tropes; the reversal of the symbolic and the semiotic; and the textual separations of history from history, self from self, body from body mentioned in the conclusion. This approach allows for detailed readings, but it can blur the larger perspective of the texts involved. Therefore, in conclusion, I would like to complement these chapters with a brief discussion of the presentation of the process of in these novels as compared

to earlier versions, specifically 's *Wilhelm Meister* and Douglass' *Narrative of the Life*.

Like most conventional European and European American *Bildungsromane*, Goethe's *Wilhelm Meister* is told by a neutral and all-knowing third person narrator who presents the maturation process of the protagonist in a flow from immaturity to maturity, a linear representation of personal and representational history. Frederick Douglass' *Narrative of the Life* and most other slave narratives break with this European style of subject presentation. For authenticity and authority, Douglass prefers to write a first person narration. The first person presentation inscribes a doubling of the subject, for the subject immediately breaks into two contingent halves. This double perspective often tends to reverse the linearity of the representation. Goethe's paradigm emphasizes a gradual unfoldment of personality (interlaced with an infoldment into a welcoming society). The African American paradigm presents an archaeological quest for being and body and thus reverses the Goethean model. The first person narrative produces an archaeological fervor: a desire to dig up the moment of birth, to reach the beginning, to understand the origin of the double subject. "I am an invisible man," Ellison's novel begins. When did I become invisible? Why did I become invisible? Who am I? How do I exist? The questions raised in the space between the subjectifier and the subjectified in the African American tradition of self-representation connect that literature with epistemological and ontological issues which tend to lead the reader in two distinct directions at once. First, it leads back to the history of African Americans in the United States and other slave-owning nations. At the same time, it heightens the self-reflexivity and underscores the artistry of the portrait.

The novels often produce this same archaeological desire in many a reader—a desire for truth, for history, for the birth of the subject and his or her development. Yet, these texts are carefully and artistically designed to thwart this desire, and thus they do much more than simply reverse the Goethean paradigm with an archaeological structure. The reader finds that the subject representation in these African American novels is neither simply an unfoldment of a personality nor simply an archaeological quest

for the birth of a subject. The double subject inscribes the beginning and
the end simultaneously, confusing both progressive and regressive models
of analysis. The double subjects in these novels change the inherent
chronology involved in the process of presenting and representing the
subject.

Being, Seeing, and Signifying the Subject

The main and most striking difference between the classical
Bildungsroman and the African American narratives of *Bildung* is located
within the creation of a double perspective on both the writing of and the
chronology of the subject. Whereas the classical *Bildungsroman* creates
the illusion that the young and inexperienced protagonist somehow
preexists the story in which he is the main feature, the African American
narrative of *Bildung* seems to suggests that life comes after the story. The
implied chronology in the classical *Bildungsroman* begins with a positing of
a Being as preexistent to text. To describe this Being the narrator aspires
to bracket all other information, to zoom in on the Being alone, to hold him
as it were in phenomenological truth in a moment of actual Seeing. This
Seeing also preexists the text. When the Seeing of the Being has taken
place, the process of Signification can begin and the reader is welcomed to
the story. These three moves are typical of the classical *Bildungsroman*.
In this classical model the narrator will posit that first there is a Being.
Through a process of bracketing the narrator can gain insight into that
Being during moments of Seeing which in turn will allow him or her to
write down the new knowledge in a process of Signifying. This structure
encourages the reader to move away from the material and historical world
into the world of art, to leap from diachrony to synchrony. It also
encourages the reader to share the illusion of untainted "Seeing."

The five African American novels I discuss are part of an African
American literary tradition that reverses the move from art to world, from
language to history, from sign to subject. Frederick Douglass' *Narrative
of the Life* is a seminal work in this tradition. The *Narrative* begins with

an introduction to the importance of language to subject formation. Douglass describes the difference between his own and other slave children's sense of self and age as compared to the white children's knowledge. He emphasizes how the white children could tell their ages and situate themselves in language, a luxury unknown to the black children. The comparison shows one way in which the slaves were excluded from written records and written history; how they were made invisible. Douglass ends the book with a moving plea for abolition of the slave system, and with this plea, he creates one of the earliest double endings in the African American tradition. These are endings that simultaneously close the book and open the world, that fuse art and history, literature and life.

Invisible man signifies on Douglass' notion of how the historical texts exclude and include black people. He begins his life story by comparing his position as a black subject-protagonist invisible to white semiotic structures like Hollywood movies and Edgar Allan Poe's novels. He concludes his long journey toward visibility with two questions: whether an invisible man also may have a socially responsible role to play and whether (on the lower frequencies) he may speak for everybody. Invisible man's contemplation of whether to end his days of underground hibernation and return to the world and his awareness that he has become a collective and representational voice both inscribe the world at the end of the novel. Beginning with art and ending with a return to the world, *Invisible Man* performs a common movement in the African American narrative of *Bildung*, a movement that reverses the inherent chronology in the classical *Bildungsroman*. Toni Morrison also provides examples of this movement. She frames the beginning of *The Bluest Eye* with a tripled quotation from the Dick-and-Jane story and ends it with a depressing view of Pecola's town where it is too late for change and an implication that maybe it is not too late to do something elsewhere. In *Oxherding Tale* Charles Johnson likewise posits the childhood world of Andrew Hawkins as "mere parable" (3) and ends with how Hawkins "turned to the business of rebuilding . . . the world" (176). *Dessa Rose* similarly opens with Dessa's memories of Kaine's touch and the things that he used to say, such as "'Don't take much, Dess—if you got the right word. And you know when it come to eating beef, I steal the right word if it ain't hiding somewhere round my own self's tongue'"(3). Dessa ends her story with a plea that her children will not have to pay the exacting price for life and freedom that Dessa's generation did: "'Oh, we have paid for our children's place in the world again, and again . . .'" (260).

All the novels I have described reverse the chronology between literature and life as it can be distilled from the classical *Bildungsroman*. The double subject of the African American narrative of *Bildung* often begins on a highly self-reflexive note, emphasizing the artistic production of signifiers and reproducing, in one fashion or another, the movement from art to history, from literature to life. The intent of this reversal, as I see it, is at the novel's end, to return the readers to their historical reality where real political changes can occur. Whereas Goethe's novel separates itself more and more from realism and concludes with an ever increasing crescendo of fantasy and fairy-tale elements, the African American narrative of *Bildung* includes a return to the real.

From the early slave narratives onward, the African American narrative of *Bildung* begins with textual comparisons and claims a temporary origin and *telos* in writing and language. Through the act of writing, the narrators of the African American narrative of *Bildung* construct a subject which is at the same time textual and historical. Existing solely in language, this self is simultaneously representational and personal.[4] These composite subjects express the need of the African American people to forge a sense of identity out of the shattering experiences of the diaspora and American slavery. But this emerging identity dramatically differs from, for example, the one idealized in the classical *Bildungsroman* and the white Western tradition. The African American identity, like the adjective that nominates it, is split. Divided between Africa and America, it is grounded in division; its geography as well as its nature is double. Comparing it to the ethnocentric classical model provides further distinctions. Wilhelm Meister, the protagonist in the classical *Bildungsroman*, transcends the cultural and historical text and improves his social status, relying on an essential inner self which allows him to overcome social and class barriers. In contrast, the subjects in the African American narrative of *Bildung* understand the degree to which they are "written" and even determined by racial, cultural, and historical "texts"; their maturation stories often deny the power of the individual to effect fundamental changes in his or her life. Yet, the African American narrative of *Bildung* is rarely a story of defeat. Writing the subject, the African American narrative of *Bildung* inverts common white and Western themes and structures, but it also effects changes in and through language.

The consistent effort to reproduce a movement from literature to life reverses the chronology in the classical *Bildungsroman*: instead of the Being-Seeing-Signifying paradigm, these African American novels begin with signifying (both in a general sense and in the ways Henry Louis Gates suggests). This signifying creates a perspective which in turn allows the reader a new kind of seeing, a seeing which is not, as in the European model, an untainted and objective mirroring of the illusive being, but rather a seeing of the very deep-structures within the signification processes which direct all readers. The African American literary tradition from the early slave narratives onward is permeated with the hope that this new seeing will create the beginnings of a new being who, hopefully, can effect changes in the social, political, and economic lives of black and white Americans. Through the processes of writing the subject, these novels exemplify the practice of text as "productive violence."[5] This constructive violence effectively describes the explicit or implicit agenda of these stories which emphasize not personal liberation, but social revolution. The African American narrative of *Bildung* returns the reader to the world at the end of the book; hopefully, the reader who has properly learned to *signify*, *see*, and *be* can reproduce in the world the effects of the subject representation in the African American narrative of *Bildung*.

NOTES

1 Amy Elias thoroughly discusses the idea of a spatialized historiography and postmodernism in *Spatializing History* (unpublished dissertation, Pennsylvania SU, 1991). See also her essay "Defining Spatial History in Postmodernist Historical Novels" in *Postmodern Studies* ed. Theo D'haen and Hans Bertens (Amsterdam: Rodopi forthcoming).

2 See my article "Approaches to Africa: The Poetics of Memory and the Body in Two August Wilson Plays," *August Wilson: A Casebook*, The Modern American Dramatists Series. Ed. Marilyn Elkins (The Garland Publishing, 1994).

3 See Julia Kristeva's *Powers of Horror: An Essay on Abjection* (Columbia UP, 1982).

4 Valerie Smith comments that "what happens to Pecola is representative, not unique." *Self-Discovery and Authority in Afro-American Narrative* (Cambridge, MA: Harvard UP) 124.

5 See Julia Kristeva (1984: 16).

SELECTED BIBLIOGRAPHY

Primary Sources

Dostoevsky, Fyodor. *Notes from Underground.* New York: Bantam Books, 1983.

Douglass, Frederick. *Narrative of the Life of Frederick Douglass, an American Slave. Written by Himself.* New York: Doubleday, 1973.

Ellison, Ralph. *Invisible Man.* New York: Vintage Books, 1972.

Goethe, Johann Wolfgang von. *Wilhelm Meister's Years of Apprenticeship*, Books I-III. Trans. H. M. Waidson. London: John Calder, 1977.

Johnson, Charles. *Oxherding Tale.* New York: Grove P, 1982.

Jones, Gayl. *Eva's Man.* Boston: Beacon P, 1987.

Morrison, Toni. *The Bluest Eye.* New York: Washington Square P, 1972.

Williams, Sherley Anne. *Dessa Rose.* New York: Berkley Books, 1986.

Secondary Sources

Abel, Elizabeth, Marianne Hirsch, and Elizabeth Langland, eds. *The Voyage In: Fictions of Female Development.* Hanover, NH: UP of New England, 1983.

——, ed. *Writing and Sexual Difference.* Chicago: U of Chicago P, 1982.

Ahmad, Aijaz. *In theory: Classes, Nations, Literatures.* London: Verso, 1992.

Alden, Patricia. *Social Mobility in the English Bildungsroman: Gissing, Hardy, Bennett, and Lawrence.* Ann Arbor: UMI Research P, 1986.

Anderson, Roger B. *Dostoevsky: Myths of Duality*. Gainesville: U of Florida P, 1986.

Arac, Jonathan, ed. *Postmodernism and Politics*. Minneapolis: U of Minnesota P, 1986.

Asante, Molefi Kete. *The Afrocentric Idea*. Philadelphia: Temple UP, 1987.

Baker, Houston A. Jr. *Blues, Ideology, and Afro-American Literature: A Vernacular Theory*. Chicago: U of Chicago P, 1984.

——. *The Journey Back: Issues in Black Literature and Criticism*. Chicago: U of Chicago P, 1980.

——. "There is No More Beautiful Way: Theory and the Poetics of Afro-American Women's Writing." *Afro-American Literary Study in the 1990s*. Ed. Houston A. Baker, Jr., and Patricia Redmond. Chicago: U of Chicago P, 1989. 135-155.

——. "When Lindbergh Sleeps with Bessie Smith: The Writing of Place in Toni Morrison's *Sula*." *The Difference Within: Feminism and Critical Theory*. Ed. Elizabeth Meese and Alice Parker. Amsterdam/Philadelphia: John Benjamins, 1989. 85-113.

Bakerman, Jane S. "Failures of Love: Female Initiation in the Novels of Toni Morrison." *American Literature* 52 (1981): 541-63.

Bakhtin, Mikhail. *The Dialogic Imagination: Four Essays*. Ed. Michael Holquist. Trans. Caryl Emerson and Michael Holquist. Austin: U of Texas P, 1981.

——. *Problems of Dostoevsky's Poetics*. Ed. and trans. Caryl Emerson. Intro. Wayne Booth. Minneapolis: U of Minnesota P, 1984.

Barksdale, Richard K. "Castration Symbolism in Recent Black American Fiction." *CLA Journal* 29 (1986): 400-413.

Barthes, Roland. *S/Z: An Essay*. Trans. Richard Miller. New York: Farrar, Straus and Giroux, 1974.

Baudrillard, Jean. *Selected Writings*. Ed. Mark Poster. Stanford: Stanford UP, 1988.

Beddow, Michael. *The Fiction of Humanity: Studies in the Bildungsroman from Wieland to Thomas Mann*. Cambridge: Cambridge UP, 1982.

Bell, Bernard W. *The Afro-American Novel and Its Tradition*. Amherst: U of Massachusetts P, 1987.

Bell, Daniel. *The Cultural Contradictions of Capitalism*. New York: Basic Books, 1976.

Bell, Roseann P., Bettye J. Parker, and Beverly Guy-Sheftall. *Sturdy Black Bridges: Visions of Black Women in Literature*. Garden City, NY: Anchor Press/Doubleday, 1979.

Belsey, Catherine and Jane Moore, eds. *The Feminist Reader: Essays in Gender and the Politics of Literary Criticism*. London: Macmillan, 1989.

Bennett, David. "Wrapping Up Postmodernism: The Subject of Consumption versus the Subject of Cognition." *Textual Practice* 1, 3 (1987): 243-261.

Benston, Kimberly W. *Speaking for You: The Vision of Ralph Ellison*. Washington, DC: Howard UP, 1987.

Bertens, Hans. "The Postmodern *Weltanschauung* and Its Relation with Modernism: An Introductory Survey." *Approaching Postmodernism: Papers Presented at a Workshop on Postmodernism, 21-23 September 1984, University of Utrecht*. Ed. Douwe Fokkema and Hans Bertens. Amsterdam/Philadelphia: John Benjamins, 1986. 9-51.

Bhabha, Homi K. *The Location of Culture*. London and New York: Routledge, 1994.

Bjork, Patrick Bryce. *The Novels of Toni Morrison: The Search for Self and Place Within the Community*. New York: Peter Lang, 1992.

Blackall, Eric A. *Goethe and the Novel*. Ithaca: Cornell UP, 1976.

Bloom, Harold, ed. *Ralph Ellison*. New York: Chelsea House, 1986.

Braendlin, Bonnie Hoover. "*Bildung* in Ethnic Women Writers." *Denver Quarterly* 17.4 (1983): 75-87.

Brenkman, John. *Culture and Domination*. Ithaca: Cornell UP, 1987.

Brooks, Peter. *Reading for the Plot: Design and Intention in Narrative*. New York: Vintage Books, 1985.

Bruford, W. H. *The German Tradition of Self-Cultivation: 'Bildung' from Humboldt to Thomas Mann*. Cambridge: Cambridge UP, 1975.

Buckley, Jerome Hamilton. *Season of Youth: The Bildungsroman from Dickens to Golding*. Cambridge, MA.: Harvard UP, 1974.

Burke, Kenneth. "Ralph Ellison's Trueblooded *Bildungsroman*." *Speaking for You: The Vision of Ralph Ellison*. Ed. Kimberley W. Benston. Washington DC: Howard UP, 1987. 349-359.

Butler-Evans, Elliott. *Race, Gender, and Desire: Narrative Strategies in the Fiction of Toni Cade Bambara, Toni Morrison, and Alice Walker*. Philadelphia: Temple UP, 1989.

Byerman, Keith E. *Fingering the Jagged Grain: Tradition and Form in Recent Black Fiction*. Athens: U of Georgia P, 1985.

——. "Intense Behaviors: The Use of the Grotesque in *The Bluest Eye* and *Eva's Man*." *CLA Journal* 25 (1982): 447-457.

Callahan, John F. *In the African-American Grain: The Pursuit of Voice in Twentieth Century Black Fiction*. Urbana: U of Illinois P, 1988.

Camus, Albert. *The Stranger*. New York: Vintage, 1946.

Carby, Hazel V. *Reconstructing Womanhood: The Emergence of the Afro-American Woman Novelist*. Oxford: Oxford UP, 1987.

Carroll, David. *The Subject in Question: The Languages of Theory and the Strategies of Fiction*. Chicago: U of Chicago P, 1982.

Cash, Earl A. "The Narrators in *Invisible Man* and *Notes from Underground*: Brothers in the Spirit." *CLA Journal* 16 (1973): 505-507.

Chatman, Seymore. *Story and Discourse: Narrative Structure in Fiction and Film*. Ithaca: Cornell UP, 1978.

Christian, Barbara. *Black Feminist Criticism: Perspectives on Black Women Writers*. New York: Pergamon, 1985.

Cixous, Hélène. *Coming to Writing and Other Essays*. Ed. Deborah Jenson. Cambridge, Mass.: Harvard UP, 1991.

——. "Sorties: Out and Out: Attacks/Ways out/Forays." *The Feminist Reader: Essays in Gender and the Politics of Literary Criticism*. Eds. Catherine Belsey and Jane Moore. New York: Blackwell, 1989.

Clark, Norris. "Flying Black: Toni Morrison's *The Bluest Eye*, *Sula* and *Song of Solomon*." *Minority Voices*, 4 (1980): 51-63.

Coleman, James W. *Blackness and Modernism: The Literary Career of John Edgar Wideman*. Jackson: UP of Mississippi, 1989.

Connor, Steven. *Postmodernist Culture: An Introduction to Theories of the Contemporary*. Oxford: Basil Blackwell, 1989.

Cooke, Michael G. *Afro-American Literature in the Twentieth Century: The Achievement of Intimacy*. New Haven: Yale UP, 1984.

Covo, Jacqueline. *The Blinking Eye: Ralph Waldo Ellison and his American, French, German and Italian Critics, 1952-1971*. Metuchen, NJ: Scarecrow, 1974.

Coward, Rosalind and John Ellis. *Language and Materialism: Developments in Semiology and the Theory of the Subject*. London: Routledge and Kegan Paul, 1977.

Currie, Peter. "The Eccentric Self: Anti-Characterization and the Problem of the Subject in American Postmodernist Fiction." *Contemporary American Fiction*. Ed. Malcolm Bradbury and Sigmund Ro. London: Edward Arnold, 1987. 53-69.

Dallmayr, Fred R. *Twilight of Subjectivity: Contributions to a Post-Individualist Theory of Politics*. Amherst: U of Massachusetts P, 1981.

Dandridge, Rita B. "Male Critics/Black Women's Novels." *CLA Journal* 32 (1979): 1-11.

Davis, Cynthia A. "Self, Society, and Myth in Toni Morrison's Fiction."
Contemporary Literature 23 (1982): 323-342.

Deleuze, Gilles and Félix Guattari. Anti-Oedipus: Capitalism and
Schizophrenia. Trans. Robert Hurley, Mark Seem, and Helen R.
Lane. Minneapolis: U of Minnesota P, 1983.

Derrida, Jacques. Of Grammatology. Trans. Gayatri Chakravorty
Spivak. Baltimore: The Johns Hopkins UP, 1974.

——. Writing and Difference. Trans. Alan Bass. Chicago: U of Chicago
P, 1978.

Deutch, Leonard J. "Ralph Waldo Ellison and Ralph Waldo Emerson: A
Shared Moral Vision." CLA Journal 16 (1972): 159-178.

Dietze, Rudolf F. Ralph Ellison: The Genesis of an Artist. Nürnberg:
Hans Carl Verlag, 1982.

Dittmar, Linda. "'Will the Circle Be Unbroken?' The Politics of Form in
The Bluest Eye." Novel 23 (2): 137-155.

Dixon, Melvin. Ride Out the Wilderness: Geography and Identity in Afro-
American Fiction. Urbana: U of Illinois P, 1987.

——. "Singing a Deep Song: Language as Evidence in the Novels of Gayl
Jones." Black Women Writers (1950-1980): A Critical Evaluation.
Ed. Mari Evans. New York: Anchor Press/Doubleday, 1984.
236-248.

Du Bois, William E. B. The Souls of Black Folk. Three Negro Classics.
New York: Avon Books, 1965. 207-389.

DuPlessis, Rachel Blau. Writing Beyond the Ending: Narrative Strategies
of Twentieth-Century Women Writers. Bloomington: Indiana UP,
1985.

Durham, Frank, ed. Studies in Cane. Columbus, OH: Charles E.
Merrill, 1971.

Eagleton, Mary, ed. Feminist Literary Theory: A Reader. Oxford: Basil
Blackwell, 1986.

Eagleton, Terry. "Capitalism, Modernism and Postmodernism." *Against the Grain: Essays 1975-1985*. London: Verso, 1986. 131-148.

——. *Literary Theory: An Introduction*. Minneapolis: U of Minnesota P, 1983.

Easthope, Antony. "Eliot, Pound, and the Subject of Postmodernism." *After the Future: Postmodern Times and Places*. Ed. Gary Shapiro. Albany: State U of New York P, 1990. 53-66.

Ellison, Ralph. *Shadow and Act*. New York: Vintage, 1972.

Fokkema, Douwe. "The Semantic and Syntactic Organization of Postmodernist Texts." *Approaching Postmodernism*. Ed. Douwe Fokkema and Hans Bertens. Amsterdam/Philadelphia: John Benjamins, 1986. 81-98.

Fogel, Robert William and Stanley L. Engerman. *Time on the Cross: The Economics of American Negro Slavery*. New York: Norton, 1974.

Foster, Hal, ed. *The Anti-Aesthetic: Essays on Postmodern Culture*. Port Townsend, WA: Bay P, 1983.

Fox, Robert Elliott. *Conscientious Sorcerers: The Black Postmodernist Fiction of LeRoi Jones/Amiri Baraka, Ishmael Reed, and Samuel R. Delany*. New York: Greenwood P, 1987.

Frank, Joseph. "Ralph Ellison and a Literary 'Ancestor': Dostoevsky," *The New Criterion* 2, 1 (1983): 11-21.

Franklin, John Hope and Alfred A. Moss, Jr. *From Slavery To Freedom: A History of Negro Americans*. New York: McGraw-Hill, 1988, 6th ed. (first ed. 1947).

Frye, Joanne S. *Living Stories, Telling Lives: Women and the Novel in Contemporary Experience*. Ann Arbor: U of Michigan P, 1986.

Gaines, Ernest J. *The Autobiography of Miss Jane Pittman*. New York: Bantam Books, 1971.

Gates, Henry Louis Jr., ed. *Black Literature and Literary Theory*. New York: Methuen, 1984.

———. *Figures in Black: Words, Signs, and the "Racial" Self.* Oxford: Oxford UP, 1987.

———, ed. *"Race," Writing, and Difference.* Chicago: U of Chicago P, 1986.

———, ed. *Reading Black, Reading Feminist: A Critical Anthology.* New York: Meridian, 1990.

———. *The Signifying Monkey: A Theory of African-American Literary Criticism.* Oxford: Oxford UP, 1988.

——— and Charles T. Davis, eds. *The Slave's Narrative.* Oxford: Oxford UP, 1985.

Gibson, Donald B., ed. *Five Black Writers: Essays on Wright, Ellison, Baldwin, Hughes, and LeRoi Jones.* New York: New York UP, 1970.

Gilbert, Sandra M. and Susan Gubar. *The Madwoman in the Attic: The Woman Writer and the Nineteenth-Century Literary Imagination.* New Haven: Yale UP, 1979.

Goldmann, Lucien. *Method in the Sociology of Literature.* Trans. and ed. William Q. Boelhower. Oxford: Blackwell, 1981.

Goodman, Charlotte. "The Lost Brother, The Twin: Women Novelists and the Male-Female *Bildungsroman. Novel* 17 (1983): 28-43.

Graff, Gerald. *Literature Against Itself: Literary Ideas in Modern Society.* Chicago: U of Chicago P, 1979.

Greene, Gayle and Coppelia Kahn, eds. *Making a Difference: Feminist Literary Criticism.* London: Routledge, 1985.

Greene, J. Lee. "The Pain and the Beauty: The South, the Black Writer, and Conventions of the Picaresque. *The American South: Portrait of a Culture.* Ed. Louis D. Rubin, Jr. Baton Rouge: Louisiana State UP, 1980. 264-288.

Gysin, Fritz. *The Grotesque in American Negro Fiction.* Bern: Francke Verlag, 1975.

Habermas, Jürgen. "Modernity versus Postmodernity," *New German Critique* 22 (Winter 1981): 3-14.

Haley, Alex. *The Autobiography of Malcolm X.* New York: Ballantine, 1965.

Harris, Trudier. *From Mammies to Militants: Domestics in Black American Literature.* Philadelphia: Temple UP, 1982.

——. *Fiction and Folklore: The Novels of Toni Morrison.* Knoxville: U of Tennessee P, 1991.

Hassan, Ihab. *Paracriticisms: Seven Speculations of the Times.* Urbana: U of Illinois P, 1975.

——. *The Postmodern Turn: Essays in Postmodern Theory and Culture.* Columbus: Ohio State UP, 1987.

——. "Prometheus as Performer: Toward a Posthumanist Culture," *Georgia Review* 31 (1977): 830-850.

Hirsch, Marianne. "The Novel of Formation as Genre: Between Great Expectations and Lost Illusions." *Genre* 12 (1979): 293-311.

——. *The Mother/Daughter Plot: Narrative, Psychoanalysis, Feminism.* Bloomington: Indiana UP, 1989.

Hogue, Lawrence W. *Discourse and the Other: The Production of the Afro-American Text.* Durham: Duke UP, 1986.

Homans, Margaret. *Bearing the Word: Language and Female Experience in Nineteenth-Century Women's Writing.* Chicago: U of Chicago P, 1986.

Howe, Susanne. *Wilhelm Meister and His English Kinsmen: Apprentices to Life.* New York: Columbia UP, 1930.

Hutcheon, Linda. *Narcissistic Narrative: The Metafictional Paradox.* Waterloo, Ontario: Wilfred Laurier UP, 1980.

——. *A Poetics of Postmodernism: History, Theory, Fiction.* London: Routledge, 1988.

——. *The Politics of Postmodernism.* London: Routledge, 1989.

Huyssen, Andreas. *After the Great Divide: Modernism, Mass Culture, Postmodernism.* Bloomington: Indiana UP, 1986.

Jackson, Blyden. *A History of Afro-American Literature*, vol. 1. Baton Rouge: Louisiana State UP, 1989.

Jakobson, Roman. "Two Aspects of Language and Two Types of Aphasic Disturbances." *Fundamentals of Language.* Ed. Roman Jakobson and Morris Halle. Leiden: Mouton's-Gravenhage, 1956. 55-82.

Jameson, Fredric. *Marxism and Form: Twentieth-Century Dialectical Theories of Literature.* Princeton: Princeton UP, 1971.

——. *The Prison-House of Language: A Critical Account of Structuralism and Russian Formalism.* Princeton: Princeton UP, 1972.

——. *The Political Unconscious: Narrative as a Socially Symbolic Act.* Ithaca: Cornell UP, 1981.

——. *Postmodernism, or, The Cultural Logic of Late Capitalism.* Durham: Duke UP, 1991.

JanMohamed, Abdul R. and David Lloyd, eds. *The Nature and Context of Minority Discourse.* Oxford: Oxford UP, 1990.

JanMohamed, Abdul R. "Negating the Negation as a Form of Affirmation in Minority Discourse: The Construction of Richard Wright as Subject." *Cultural Critique* 7 (Fall 1987): 245-266.

Johnson, Barbara. *The Critical Difference: Essays in the Contemporary Rhetoric of Reading.* Baltimore: The Johns Hopkins UP, 1980.

——. "Is Female to Male as Ground Is to Figure?" *Feminism and Psychoanalysis.* Ed. Richard Feldstein and Judith Roof. Ithaca: Cornell UP, 1989. 255-268.

——. *A World of Difference.* Baltimore: The Johns Hopkins UP, 1987.

Johnson, Charles. *Being and Race: Black Writing since 1970.* Bloomington: Indiana UP, 1990.

——. *Middle Passage.* New York: Atheneum, 1990.

Johnson, James Weldon. *The Autobiography of an Ex-Colored Man.* *Three Negro Classics.* New York: Avon Books, 1965. 391-511.

Johnston, John. "Ideology, Representation, Schizophrenia: Toward a Theory of the Postmodern Subject." *After the Future: Postmodern Times and Places.* Ed. Gary Shapiro. Albany: SU of New York P, 1990. 67-95.

Kaplan, E. Ann, ed. *Postmodernism and Its Discontents: Theories, Practices.* London: Verso, 1988.

Kauffman, Linda, ed. *Gender and Theory: Dialogues on Feminist Criticism.* Oxford: Basil Blackwell, 1989.

Kester, Gunilla Theander. "The Forbidden Apple and Female Disorderly Eating: Three Versions of Eve." *Disorderly Eaters: Texts in Self-Empowerment*, Eds. Lilian R. Furst and Peter W. Graham. Pennsylvania State UP, 1992.

——. "Approaches to Africa: The Poetics of Memory and the Body in Two August Wilson Plays." *August Wilson: A Casebook*, Ed. Marilyn Elkins. New York: Garland P, 1994.

Klotman, Phyllis R. "Dick-and-Jane and the Shirley Temple Sensibility in *The Bluest Eye.*" *Black American Literature Forum* 13 (1979): 123-125.

Kristeva, Julia. *Revolution in Poetic Language.* New York: Columbia UP, 1984.

——. *The Kristeva Reader.* Ed. Toril Moi. New York: Columbia UP, 1986.

Kroker, Arthur and David Cook. *The Postmodern Scene: Excremental Culture and Hyper-Aesthetics.* New York: St. Martin's P, 1988.

Kundera, Milan. *The Joke.* New York: Harper Perennial, 1992.

Labovitz, Esther Kleinbord. *The Myth of the Heroine: The Female Bildungsroman in the Twentieth Century : Dorothy Richardson, Simone de Beauvoir, Doris Lessing, Christa Wolf.* New York: Peter Lang, 1986.

Lee, Alison. *Realism and Power: Postmodern British Fiction.* London: Routledge, 1990.

Lee, Robert A., ed. Black Fiction: New Studies in the Afro-American Novel Since 1945. London: Vision P, 1980.

Leitch, Vincent B. *Deconstructive Criticism: An Advanced Introduction.* New York: Columbia UP, 1983.

Lemon, Lee T. and Marion J. Reis, eds. *Russian Formalist Criticism: Four Essays.* Lincoln: U of Nebraska P, 1965.

LeSeur, Geta. "One Mother, Two Daughters: The Afro-American and the Afro-Caribbean Female *Bildungsroman.*" *The Black Scholar* 17, 2 (1986): 26-33.

Lindberg, Gary. *The Confidence Man in American Literature.* Oxford: Oxford UP, 1982.

List, Robert N. *Dedalus in Harlem: The Joyce-Ellison Connection.* Washington DC: UP of America, Inc., 1982.

Lodge, David. "The Language of Modernist Fiction: Metaphor and Metonymy." *Modernism 1890-1930.* Ed. Malcolm Bradbury and James McFarlane. London: Penguin, 1976. 481-496.

——. *The Modes of Modern Writing: Metaphor, Metonymy, and the Typology of Modern Literature.* Ithaca: Cornell UP, 1977.

Lukács, Georg. "Das Ideal des harmonischen Menchen in der Bürgerlichen Ästhetic." *Essays Über Realismus.* Berlin: Hermann Luchterhand Verlag, 1971. 299-311.

——. "The Ideology of Modernism." *Twentieth Century Literary Criticism: A Reader.* Ed. David Lodge. London: Longman, 1972. 474-487.

——. *The Theory of the Novel: A Historico-Philosophical Essay on the Forms of Great Epic Literature.* Cambridge, MA.: The MIT P, 1987.

Lyotard, Jean-Francois. *The Postmodern Condition: A Report on Knowledge.* Trans. Geoff Bennington and Brian Massumi. Foreword Fredric Jameson. Minneapolis: U of Minnesota P, 1984.

Malmgren, Carl D. "'From Work to Text': The Modernist and Postmodernist *Künstlerroman*." *Novel* 21, 1 (1987): 5-28.

Marshall, Paule. *The Chosen Place, The Timeless People*. New York: Vintage, 1992 (first ed. 1969).

Martin, Wallace. *Recent Theories of Narrative*. Ithaca: Cornell UP, 1986.

Martini, Fritz. "Der Bildungsroman, Zur Geschichte des Wortes und der Theorie." *Deutsche Vierteljahresschrift für Literaturwissenschaft*, 35, 1961.

McConnell, Frank D. "Black Words and Black Becoming." *Yale Review* 63 (1974): 193-210.

McDowell, Deborah E. and Arnold Rampersad, eds. *Slavery and the Literary Imagination*. Baltimore: The Johns Hopkins UP, 1989.

McHale, Brian. *Postmodernist Fiction*. New York: Methuen, 1987.

McKay, Nellie Y. *Critical Essays on Toni Morrison*. Boston: G.K. Hall, 1988.

McSweeney, Kerry. *Invisible Man: Race and Identity*. Boston: Twayne Publishers, 1988.

Meese, Elizabeth A. *Crossing the Double-Cross: The Practice of Feminist Criticism*. Chapel Hill: U of North Carolina P, 1986.

—— and Alice Parker. *The Difference Within: Feminism and Critical Theory*. Amsterdam/Philadelphia: John Benjamins, 1989.

Meese, Elizabeth A. *(Ex)tensions: Re-Figuring Feminist Criticism*. Urbana: U of Illinois P, 1990.

Mellard, James M. *The Exploded Form: The Modernist Novel in America*. Urbana: U of Illinois P, 1980.

Menhennet, Alan. *Order and Freedom: Literature and Society in Germany from 1720 to 1805*. New York: Basic Books, Inc., 1973.

Miles, David H. *Hofmannsthal's Novel Andreas: Memory and Self*. Princeton: Princeton UP, 1972.

Miller, J. Hillis. *The Linguistic Moment: From Wordsworth to Stevens*. Princeton: Princeton UP, 1985.

Moi, Toril. *Sexual/Textual Politics: Feminist Literary Theory*. New York: Methuen, 1985.

Moretti, Franco. *The Way of the World: The Bildungsroman in European Culture*. London: Verso, 1987.

Morrison, Toni. *Beloved*. New York: Knopf, 1987.

——. *Playing in the Dark: Whiteness and the Literary Imagination*. New York: Vintage Books, 1993.

——. *Conversations with Toni Morrison*. Ed. Danille Taylor-Guthrie. Jackson: UP of Mississippi, 1994.

Nadal, Alan. *Invisible Criticism: Ralph Ellison and the American Canon*. Iowa City: U of Iowa P, 1988.

Newman, Charles. *The Post-Modern Aura: The Act of Fiction in an Age of Inflation*. Evanston: Northwestern UP, 1985.

Ngugi wa Thiong'o. *Decolonizing the Mind: The Politics of Language in African Literature*. London: J. Currey, 1986.

Nicholson, Linda J., ed. *Feminism/Postmodernism*. London: Routledge, 1990.

Nisula, Dasha Culic. "Dostoevski and Richard Wright: From St. Petersburg to Chicago." *Dostoevski and the Human Condition after a Century*. Ed. Alexej Ugrinsky, Frank S. Lambasa, and Valija K. Ozolins. New York: Greenwood P, 1986. 163-170.

Norris, Christopher. *Deconstruction: Theory and Practice*. New York: Methuen, 1982.

O'Brien, John. *Interviews with Black Writers*. New York: Liveright, 1973.

Olney, James. "The Founding Fathers—Frederick Douglass and Booker T. Washington." *Slavery and the Literary Imagination*. Ed. Deborah E. McDowell and Arnold Rampersad. Baltimore: The Johns Hopkins UP. 1-24.

Oloffson, Tommy. *Frigörelse eller sammanbrott; Stephen Dedalus, Martin Birck och psykologin.* Stockholm: Wahlström och Widstrand, 1981.

Omans, Stuart E. "The Variations on a Masked Leader: A Study of the Literary Relationship of Ralph Ellison and Herman Melville." *South Atlantic Bulletin* 40 (1975): 15-23.

O'Meally, Robert. *The Craft of Ralph Ellison.* Cambridge, MA.: Harvard UP, 1980.

——, ed. *New Essays on Invisible Man.* Cambridge: Cambridge UP, 1988.

O'Neale, Sondra. "Race, Sex and Self: Aspects of *Bildung* in Select Novels by Black American Women Novelists." *Melus* 9, 4 (1982): 25-37.

Perloff, Marjorie, ed. *Postmodern Genres.* Norman: U of Oklahoma P, 1989.

Petesch, Donald A. *A Spy in the Enemy's Country: The Emergence of Modern Black Literature.* Iowa City: U of Iowa P, 1989.

Plato. *The Republic.* London: Penguin Books, 1987.

Pratt, Annis, ed. *Archetypal Patterns in Women's Fiction.* Bloomington: Indiana UP, 1981.

Radhakrisnan, R. "Ethnic Identity and Poststructuralist Differance." *The Nature and Context of Minority Discourse.* Ed. Abdul JanMohamed and David Lloyd. Oxford: Oxford UP, 1990. 50-71

Rashdy, Ashraf H. A. "Reading Mammy: The Subject of Relation in Sherley Anne Williams' *Dessa Rose.*" *African American Review* 27 (1993): 365-89.

——. "The Phenomenology of the Allmuseri: Charles Johnson and the Subject of the Narrative of Slavery." *African American Review* 26 (1992): 373-94.

Robinson, Sally. *Gender and Self-Representation in Contemporary Women's Fiction.* SU of New York P, 1991.

Rodnon, Stewart. *"The Adventures of Huckleberry Finn* and *Invisible Man*: Thematic and Structural Comparisons." *Black American Literature Forum* 4 (1970): 45-51.

Romberg, Bertil. *Studies in the Narrative Technique of the First-Person Novel.* Stockholm: Almqvist Wiksell, 1962.

Ross, Andrew, ed. *Universal Abandon? The Politics of Postmodernism.* Minneapolis: U of Minnesota P, 1988.

Rovit, Earl H. "Ralph Ellison and the American Comic Tradition." *Wisconsin Studies in Contemporary Literature* 1 (1960): 34-42.

Rowell, Charles H. "An Interview with Gayl Jones." *Callaloo* 3 (1982): 32-53.

Rubinstein, Roberta. *Boundaries of the Self: Gender, Culture, Fiction.* Urbana: U of Illinois P, 1987.

Saussure, Ferdinand de. *Course in General Linguistics.* Ed. Charles Bally, Albert Sechehaye, and Albert Reidlinger. Trans. Wade Baskin. London: Fontana/Collins, 1974.

Sax, Benjamin C. *Images of Identity: Goethe and the Problem of Self-Conception in the Nineteenth Century.* New York: Peter Lang, 1987.

Scholes, Robert. *Structuralism in Literature: An Introduction.* New Haven: Yale UP, 1974.

Scruggs, Charles W. "Ralph Ellison's Use of *The Aeneid* in *Invisible Man.*" *CLA Journal* 17 (1974): 368-78.

Searle, John R. *Expression and Meaning: Studies in the Theory of Speech Acts.* Cambridge: Cambridge UP, 1979.

Shaeffer, Jean-Marie. "Literary Genres and Textual Genricity." *The Future of Literary Theory.* Ed. Ralph Cohen. New York: Routledge, 1989. 167-187.

Shaffner, Randolph P. *The Apprenticeship Novel: A Study of the "Bildungsroman" as a Regulative Type in Western Literature with a Focus on Three Classic Representatives by Goethe, Maughan, and Mann.* New York: Peter Lang, 1984.

Shapiro, Gary, ed. *After the Future: Postmodern Times and Places.* New York: SU of New York P, 1990.

Shockley, Ann Allen. "The Black Lesbian in American Literature: An Overview." *Conditions* 5 (1979): 133-142.

Showalter, Elaine. "Feminist Criticism in the Wilderness." *Writing and Sexual Difference.* Ed. Elizabeth Abel. Chicago: U Chicago P, 1982. 9-35.

Silverman, Hugh, J., ed. *Postmodernism—Philosophy and the Arts.* New York: Routledge, 1990.

Silverman, Kaja. *The Subject of Semiotics.* Oxford: Oxford UP, 1983.

Smith, Paul. *Discerning the Subject.* Minneapolis: U of Minnesota P, 1988.

Smith, Valerie. *Self-Discovery and Authority in Afro-American Narrative.* Cambridge, MA.: Harvard UP, 1987.

Spanos, William V. *Repetitions: The Postmodern Occasion in Literature and Culture.* Baton Rouge: Louisiana State UP, 1987.

Spivak, Gayatri Chakravorty. *The Post-Colonial Critic: Interviews, Strategies, Dialogues.* Ed. Sarah Harasym. New York: Routledge, 1990.

Stahl, Ernst Ludwig. *Die religiöse und die humanitätsphilosophische Bildungsidee und die Entstehung des deutschen Bildungsroman im 18. Jahrhundert.* Bern: n.p., 1934.

Stepto, Robert B. *From Behind the Veil: A Study of Afro-American Narrative.* Urbana: U of Illinois P, 1979.

Suleiman, Susan Rubin, ed. *The Female Body in Western Culture: Contemporary Perspectives.* Cambridge, MA: Harvard UP, 1986.

——. *Subversive Intent: Gender, Politics, and the Avant-Garde.* Cambridge, MA: Harvard UP, 1990.

Swales, Martin. *The German Bildungsroman from Wieland to Hesse.* Princeton: Princeton UP, 1978.

Tate, Claudia C., ed. *Black Women Writers at Work.* New York: Continuum, 1988.

——. "An Interview with Gayl Jones." *Black American Literature Forum* 13: 142-48.

Todorov, Tzvetan. *Mikhail Bakhtin: The Dialogical Principle.* Trans. Wlad Godzich. Minneapolis: U of Minnesota P, 1984.

Tomashevsky, Boris. "Thematics." *Russian Formalist Criticism: Four Essays.* Ed. and trans. Lee T. Lemon and Marion J. Reis. Lincoln: U of Nebraska P, 1965.

Toomer, Jean. *Cane.* New York: Liveright, 1975.

Wall, Cheryl A., ed. *Changing Our Own Words: Essays on Criticism, Theory, and Writing by Black Women.* New Brunswick: Rutgers UP, 1989.

Wallace, Michele. *Invisibility Blues: From Pop to Theory.* London: Verso, 1990.

Ward, Jr., Jerry W. "Escape from Trublem: The Fiction of Gayl Jones." *Callaloo* 5 (1982): 95-111.

Waugh, Patricia. *Feminine Fictions: Revisiting the Postmodern.* London: Routledge, 1989.

Weever, Jacqueline de. "The Inverted World of Toni Morrison's *The Bluest Eye* and *Sula*." *CLA Journal* 22 (1979): 402-414.

Weinstein, Philip M. *The Semantics of Desire: Changing Models of Identity from Dickens to Joyce.* Princeton: Princeton UP, 1984.

West, Cornel. *Keeping Faith: Philosophy and Race in America.* New York: Routledge, 1993.

Williams, Sherley Anne. *Give Birth to Brightness: A Thematic Study in Neo-Black Literature*. New York: The Dial P, 1972.

Willis, Susan. *Specifying: Black Women Writing the American Experience*. Madison: U of Wisconsin P, 1987.

Wilson, August. *Three Plays*. Pittsburg: U of Pittsburg P, 1991.

Wright, Richard. "The Man Who Lived Underground." *Eight Men*. Rpr. New York: Thunder's Mouth P, 1987.

Yaeger, Patricia. *Honey-Mad Women: Emancipatory Strategies in Women's Writing*. New York: Columbia UP, 1988.

Yúdice, George. "Marginality and the Ethics of Survival." *Universal Abandon? The Politics of Postmodernism*. Ed. Andrew Ross. Minneapolis: U of Minnesota P, 1988. 214-236.

INDEX

A

A Farewell to Arms, 9

A Portrait of the Artist as a Young Man, 91

Abel, Elizabeth, 96, 105

Africa, 13, 16, 27, 42, 110, 127, 131, 148

agency, 11–12, 14–15, 18, 30, 79

Alden, Patricia, 10, 20, 52

Anbildung, 8, 97

Anti-Oedipus, 45

Aristotle, 11, 75, 139

Armstrong, Louis, 1, 24

Ausbildung, 8, 97–98

Austen, Jane, 91

authenticity, 137, 145

autobiography, 7, 93

B

Baker, Houston, 13

Bakhtin, Mikhail M., 30, 33, 35, 123, 138

Baldwin, James, 111

Bambara, Toni Cade, 71

Barksdale, Richard K., 79

Barthes, Roland, 46–47, 104

Baudrillard, Jean, 90, 105

Beddow, Michael, 7, 71

Being and Race, 111–112

Bell, Bernard, 72

Bell, Daniel, 14

Beloved, 141, 143

Bertens, Hans, 14, 150

Bildung,

    African American female narrative of, 73–98

    African American narrative of, 5–19, 21–39, 45–70, 107–134, 144–149

    female narrative of, 104

    process of, 1, 8–18, 30–39, 46–52, 60–69, 75, 92–97, 107–127, 144

Bildungsroman, 5–19, 20, 21–24, 28–30, 38–39, 42, 45–69, 90–96, 140–149

    female, 91, 96, 104

Bjork, Patrick Bryce, 98

Black Boy, 9

Blackall, Eric, 7

blackness, 1–3, 18, 22–36, 105, 108–131, 133, 140, 143

blood, 2, 27, 85, 102, 127–132

blues, the, 13, 37, 61, 73, 93, 139

body, 26, 34, 42, 45, 73, 81–87, 102, 103, 108–113, 118–125, 129, 135, 137–138, 142–144

Borges, Jorge Luis, 45